I0472151

HOW TO BE A ROCK STAR REALTOR

HOW TO BE A ROCK STAR REALTOR

TARA WINFREE

© 2017 Tara Winfree
All rights reserved.

ISBN-13: 9781540489814
ISBN-10: 1540489817
Library of Congress Control Number: 2016919583
CreateSpace Independent Publishing Platform
North Charleston, South Carolina

CONTENTS

Preface ·vii

Chapter 1 7 x 7 = Success ·1
Chapter 2 Real Estate GPS · 11
Chapter 3 Prospecting· 14
Chapter 4 Elevator Speech· 17
Chapter 5 Market Knowledge · · · · · · · · · · · · · · · · · · ·20
Chapter 6 Don't Confuse Activity with Results· · · · · · · · · · ·22
Chapter 7 Maintaining a Database · · · · · · · · · · · · · · · · ·24
Chapter 8 Time and Money ·28
Chapter 9 Find Your Way ·31
Chapter 10 Positive Thoughts ·34
Chapter 11 Time Management ·37
Chapter 12 Plan Every Day· ·40
Chapter 13 Stress Management· · · · · · · · · · · · · · · · · · · ·43
Chapter 14 80/20 and You ·46
Chapter 15 No Longer for Sale ·49
Chapter 16 Facebook· ·54

Chapter 17 Farming ·59
Chapter 18 For Sale by Owner · · · · · · · · · · · · · · · · · · ·65
Chapter 19 Open Houses ·69
Chapter 20 Values Statement· ·75
Chapter 21 The Referral Game · · · · · · · · · · · · · · · · · · ·77
Chapter 22 The Wide World· ·80
Chapter 23 More Than Prospecting · · · · · · · · · · · · · · · ·83
Chapter 24 Practice, Practice, Practice· · · · · · · · · · · · · · ·85
Chapter 25 Letting the Client Win · · · · · · · · · · · · · · · · ·88
Chapter 26 The Lie ·92
Chapter 27 When the Seller Has Cold Feet· · · · · · · · · · · · ·95
Chapter 28 Do Ask for It ·99

            Addendum · 107
            Conclusion · 115
            References· 117

PREFACE

When it comes to real estate, you could say that I have been around the block. I am a second-generation Realtor (and maybe even a third-generation Realtor, since my grandparents started scooping up land during the Depression). I have been a top producer, I have run a real estate marketing department, I have been a managing broker, and I have been a coach for a national real estate coaching company. I have met with hundreds of agents. This book is not just a compilation of my thoughts but proven wisdom that hundreds of agents have followed to success.

This is *not* a case of the emperor with no clothes. This is the truth: it works, it has worked, and it will work. The funny thing about real estate is that it is not rocket science; it is more a tried-and-true business. There are certain ways to beat the pavement for business that work. And for the most part, every coaching company preaches the same methods with a different twist. I like to say that we all have the same mannequin; we just have different clothes and accessories to put on the mannequin. The same holds true for your business. In real estate, we all have the same basic free tools, but it is what you do and how you do it that accessorize your mannequin into a winning one or a losing one.

Unfortunately, in real estate, there are two types of Realtors: winners and losers. You either make it in the business (and you tend to make it big), or you don't. The dropout rate is high—about the same as the restaurant failure rate. I want you to be a winner. I want you to succeed at this business. I know you can, you know you can, and my hope is that this book will lead you down the right path to get to the other side of this small patch of woods in which you are lost. The winner's meadow is large, not very crowded, and ready for you. What are you waiting for?

Chapter 1

7 X 7 = SUCCESS

It's a wonderful time to be selling real estate. Truthfully, anytime is a wonderful time to be selling real estate. As long as people are working, getting married, having kids, getting divorced, dying, getting laid off—as long as life is happening—people will be buying and selling real estate. Real estate was sold even in the Great Depression. Can money be made selling real estate? Absolutely. No college degree is required; with a working knowledge of the contract and some sales skills, you can make it big as a Realtor.

The problem with being a Realtor is that there are so many ways to be successful—so many different theories and approaches—that you are actually drowning in options or being sucked into options like quicksand pulls in a fighting human. The more you resist, the more companies try to sell you and the more another agent in your office claims his or her way is best. The more you hear, the faster you sink until you are left unable to implement what *you* want to grow your business.

There is a solution. You became a Realtor because you wanted to be your own boss. You wanted to do things your way. Now it is time to do it your way. To be honest, it doesn't matter what you do as long as you are doing a money-generating activity every day (more on this later). Are you ready to get on with your business and become the entrepreneur you know you can be and make the money you want?

STEP ONE: BE SELECTIVE

As I mentioned, you have many options to generate business. You could never do all of them yourself. And doing all of them partially won't help you generate leads, and leads turn into appointments, and appointments turn into yeses. Yeses turn into money.

Pick a couple of ways to generate business and then stick to them. Consistency is the name of the game. When it comes to marketing and real estate, it almost doesn't matter what you do as long as you do it consistently. Doing it once will not work.

Many times, agents jump into the latest and newest fad and try it once. But when nothing happens, they never do it again. They waste hundreds of dollars trying it once.

The rule of seven is an old marketing adage that says until potential prospects see your message seven times, they aren't even aware they saw it. In other words, the first seven times you send a postcard or e-mail, all you do is make an impression. The prospect will not remember your name or message. After seven impressions (e-mails, postcards, etc.), your name and message will sound familiar. Does that mean on impression seven or eight the prospect will suddenly call you? Absolutely not. But it does mean that the probability of a prospect calling you or remembering that you are in real estate after one contact is about 2 percent.

The same rule applies when it comes to directional signs. Have you ever noticed that top agents have directions with their names and numbers on the signs? When you have a listing and put up directionals, you do it for two reasons. The first is to direct prospective buyers to your listing. The second, and more important reason, is to make your seven impressions on the neighbors so that if they are thinking of selling, then they can call you.

Every time a neighbor drives by your directional and glances at the sign, it is an impression. Remember, it takes seven impressions before people even realize they have seen your name before. Fill a neighborhood where you have a listing with personally branded directional signs. Before you know it, neighbors will start telling you "I see your name everywhere I go." What they are seeing are your directional signs every time they drive in and out of their street. If potential prospects think they see your name everywhere they go, then they assume you are successful. Success breeds success.

When a new restaurant opens up in town and gets a good review, you are willing to wait for a table. Heck, in DC, you might have to make a reservation six months in advance. (I did this once, and by the time the date rolled around, I totally forgot and missed my reservation!) But you do it. You wait an hour and a half for a table at a crowded restaurant instead of driving two blocks to a less popular restaurant with no wait. Why? Because success breeds success. As humans, we instinctively migrate to where other humans are. We follow the crowd. When we talk about teenagers, we call it peer pressure. As adults, we follow the same behavior. Do you remember the *Candid Camera* TV show? In one episode, a group of people is on an elevator. One person turns around backward (for no reason), and before you know it, everyone is riding the elevator facing the back instead of the doors. This is a classic human response. We don't always need to know why, but we figure that if someone else is doing it, then so should we. Did your mother ever say to you "If your friends jump off a bridge, are you going to?" She was referencing the need to follow, the need to do what others are doing.

But it isn't just restaurants. We do it with hair salons, dentists, gas stations, and the like. I once sat in line for thirty minutes to get my oil changed. The entire time I was in line, I was looking out my window at a gas station across the street that performed oil changes with no line. Why was I sitting in line? I assumed the other place was overpriced, had been accused of bad performance, or had some other reason why no one was there. It never dawned on me that maybe no one had broken the mold and tried the other gas station. Maybe there was no reason that no one was at that gas station.

In your real estate career, don't be the empty gas station. Be the one with the line. How? By creating the appearance that you are successful and busy, and everybody who is anybody is using you. Do it by repetition, by consistency. Whatever marketing drum you beat, beat it often, and beat it loud. What drums can you beat?

As previously mentioned, getting branded directionals and open house signs are a must as soon as your budget permits. When you first start out in real estate, money may be tight, and you don't have any listings. But as the wheel of business gets going, invest in yourself and your business by using personalized signs. Remember, it's about impressions. Yes, signs will get taken down, removed by the Department of Transportation, stolen, and who knows what else, and yes, it costs money to replace them—but a listing is worth the cost of a few signs. According to the National Association of Realtors, every time a home sells, seven people in a 250-home radius consider selling, and one of them will. Are you connecting with those potential sellers? The most passive way to make the connection with the next potential seven sellers in a neighborhood is via personalized directional signs. How many should you put out? You should put out enough signs to thoroughly cover a 250-home radius and get the needed seven impressions so that the potential seller thinks of calling you. (In many neighborhoods and jurisdictions, there is a limit to the number of signs you can put out, so please be aware of your local rules and regulations.)

FARMING

Mailings may be old-fashioned, but they are a tried-but-true method. As postage continues to rise, fewer Realtors are mailing, which means that when you do mail, you are more likely to stand out. *The key to farming is to mail often, and mail something of value.*

At the time of this writing, first-class postage is forty-seven cents, so many of you are shaking in your shoes at the thought of using the post office. But you can now mail by mail carrier route via the post office program Every Door Direct Mail, which brings the cost down to about seventeen cents a postcard. Here in Reston, Virginia, a mail carrier route will usually give you a mix of single family homes, townhomes, and a few condos, which is the ideal mix for farming.

As previously mentioned, the key is to mail often, do it consistently, and make sure you do it more than seven times. What do you mail? If you have listings in your farm area, then send a just-listed postcard, an under contract postcard, and a just-sold postcard for every listing in your farm. You can't brag about your success enough. Agents often think that they are bragging and feel uncomfortable, but no one notices the bragging but other agents. To the general public, it is just a blip on their radar. If you don't stay in front of them, then they forget you.

Each postcard will be read for two seconds—yes, two seconds—so don't put a lot of words on the postcard, but do use pictures.

What can you send besides just-listed and just-sold cards? The one thing all homeowners want to know is the value of their homes. For most people, owning a home is a large portion of their financial portfolio. When you own stock or have a financial adviser, you receive quarterly statements about your investments. Your bank sends you monthly statements about your accounts. But other than the county tax assessment bill, homeowners do not receive any update telling them the value of their homes. If they read the local or regional newspaper, then one day it says the market is up and the next it says the market is crashing. It is like relying on the business section to know what your personal stock portfolio is doing, which is a very unreliable way to get personalized news. A homeowner might then turn to Zillow to see their zestimate. As Realtors, we all know that a zestimate is just that, a guess with a Z in front of it. A logarithm is used to calculate a home's value. The fine print on the Zillow website says that it may not be accurate, but sellers don't see that. As a Realtor, you can provide value by telling people what their homes are worth. How? Send quarterly neighborhood statistics showing what price their neighbors' homes sold for and when. Use pictures. In other words, do a neighborhood comparative market analysis. Place the information on a postcard and then print it, and put it in an envelope. If you do use an envelope, then consider printing on the outside of the envelope "Your Neighborhood Market Update" or "Open Me to Find Out What Your Home Is Worth"—something to get the envelope opened. Remember to be consistent. If you decide to do this, then do it every quarter. Doing it hit or miss does not build trust or show knowledge.

What else can you mail? You can mail anything that says you are a successful real estate agent. Send just-listed cards, even if the listing isn't in the farm neighborhood. Some agents like to send recipe cards, others prefer a calendar of events, some like home tips, and others prefer positive quotes. Another option is to do a newsletter: you can offer market statistic articles about home ownership, feature a home that someone in your farm might aspire to move to, or provide a calendar of events. Consider a contest: "Guess the price this home will sell for and win tickets to the local theater" or "Enter a drawing to win tickets to a local charity ball." Make it local, make it fun, and make it enticing so that you capture their information.

At the end of the day, if the mailing is consistently branded and allows impressions to be made, then it almost doesn't matter what is on the mailing. Pick something, and do it!

E-CARDS

When it comes to e-cards, use the same philosophy as farming. Send something on a regular basis. According to Campaign Monitor, 92 percent of online adults use e-mail, so why wouldn't you? In fact, if you send an e-mail campaign four times a month, then you have a greater chance of someone opening one of those e-mails, according to WhoIsHostingThis.com (2014).

Include items of importance, such as customized neighborhood home values. The secret is lots of color, few words (like a postcard), and something that can be absorbed quickly—a short, concise message before the delete button is hit. Consider sending a happy holidays message, a fun image for the season, or a homeowners' joke message—something that makes people smile in the few seconds they see it, something that feels personalized to the receiver, and something that is clearly branded to you.

One e-card idea that usually receives a reply is a happy anniversary card. After you return from settlement and as you are closing out the file, take the time to generate a one-year anniversary e-card, and schedule it to be sent in exactly one year. Sellers love it and usually share it with their friends. You can also schedule quarterly house tip e-mails to go to the purchaser, such as "don't forget to turn off your outside water," and "trim the trees so they don't touch the roof." If you really want to impress your clients, take a few minutes to thumb through the home inspection report and pick a couple of maintenance items the home inspector noted, then schedule the e-mail to be sent at the appropriate time of year. Send birthday e-cards as well. If you know the kids' birthdays, then that is even better.

> If you really want to impress your clients, take a few minutes to thumb through the home inspection report and pick a couple of maintenance items the home inspector noted, then schedule the e-mail to be sent at the appropriate time of year.

E-cards that are more generic will also produce a reaction. The key to e-mail marketing is to remember that silence is not a no. In fact, most people read an e-mail and delete it; they don't reply or say anything. For those of us in sales, silence feels like a no. But in the land of e-mail, unless someone asks you to stop e-mailing them or opts out of a campaign, silence is a way of consenting to receipt of the e-mail. So don't stop, but be careful not to send too many e-mails. Try to keep it to once or twice a month; otherwise, it becomes annoying.

E-NEWSLETTERS

Similar to e-cards, an e-newsletter is sent via e-mail once a month for the best results. What do you put in an e-newsletter? You can include the same type of thing you would put in a print newsletter, such as market statistics, links to articles about home ownership, teases to move up homes, and a calendar of events. You know your target audience best. You know how you are trying to brand yourself. Be true to your branding. If you are a horse-and-country agent, then sending a newsletter about nightclubs in a nearby city may not match your marketing image. But sending a newsletter about horse shows and horse properties would match your marketing image. If you have the time to segment your audience and send specific messaging, then you are going to increase your bang for your e-mail by 760 percent, according to Campaign Monitor.

Make sure you have a call to action in every piece (this goes for an e-card as well). Human beings need to be told what to do; the subtle implication does not work well in sales. But your call to action can be creative, such as "What are the five things your next home has to have? Click here." The link would be to a survey or social media post. Ideally, do a call-to-action button rather than a link for greater results. But if in doubt, then a link is better than nothing.

An agent recently told me her e-newsletter included a tidbit about how to buy a home, information about how to sell a home, and something about how to maintain a home. She sent that once a month until she got too busy to keep it up.

Be consistent about when you send your newsletter. I used to send mine on the fifteenth of the month like clockwork. When I stopped sending it, I actually received e-mails from a couple of people asking me where my newsletter was. Provide useful information on a consistent basis, and people will become used to the information and identify with you as a real estate expert.

Whatever schedule you pick, commit to doing it seven times so that you see results. Repetition is key. Thousands of people every day respond to advertising in the forms mentioned in this chapter. If done right, then they will respond to you.

I should mention that subject lines for both e-cards and e-newsletters are key. According to Campaign Monitor, 66 percent of adults decide if they are going to open an e-mail based on the subject line. Put the person's first name in the subject line and then something enticing. Be creative, provoke interest, and be informative without giving too much away. For example, "Tara, hoping to help" or "Tara, I have been thinking about your next home."

Chapter 2

REAL ESTATE GPS

As you look back over the past twelve months, did you do as well as you had hoped? If not, then like a diet, we can start again tomorrow, and we can be as successful as we had hoped—but we have to be committed. We have to put the time and effort into our business and ourselves.

MAKE A PLAN

I know the sound of a business plan is downright scary to most of us. We are Realtors, not business planners. But the truth is that if you don't know where you are going, then you are never going to get there. Let's say, for example, that I asked you to drive from Reston, Virginia, to New Cumberland, West Virginia, but you could not use a map, a GPS, your cell phone, or anything else that would tell you how to get there—and you had just twenty-four hours to do it. Could you do it? Perhaps, but it would be a long, painful journey with lots of stops to ask for directions. And of course, no two people would give you the same directions. Most of us wouldn't make it; in fact, most of us would give up. Your real estate career is no different. Without a business plan, it is like driving without a road map or GPS. How will you know where you are going? How will you know what you need to do to achieve your goals? It's great to say that you want to make $50,000 or $100,000 or $200,000 in real estate, but *how* is the question. How many homes do you need to sell in a month to reach your goal? (Average the homes you sold this year times your average commission times your split divided by your monthly income goal; this equals how many homes you need to sell.) Assuming you know that, how many deals do you need to have in the pipeline to hit that number? (Always assume that at least one will go belly up, but if you are working divorces, short sales, and the like, then your fall-through number may be higher.) Let's say that you need to be working four deals a month to ensure three settlements a month. How many clients do you need to talk to a month? Not every listing appointment turns into a listing, so maybe every two out of three turns into a listing. Now you need to go on six listing appointments to try and get four under contract, hoping that three make it to the table.

Have I lost you? Don't worry; it's not rocket science. It's a numbers game, one that you are good at. Not every deal will settle. Not every client will go under contract. Not every listing will get an offer. Not every person you talk to will hire you. And all of that is fine; it's part of the business. What isn't fine is not knowing how many people you need to talk to or how many deals you need to put together to get to where you want to go. Hoping it happens and expecting every deal to make it to the table is not how you spell success in real estate. *Having enough fishing rods in the lake to catch more fish than you need is how you achieve your goal.*

Learn your numbers, and start working them. Knowing you need two settlements a month and focusing on that number will drive you to do the activities that will generate success. And to go back to my opening analogy, now that you have a map and an exact address, plug it into your GPS, and follow the directions. Now that you know where you are going, the rest is easy (that's step two, in case you were wondering).

Chapter 3

PROSPECTING

As Realtors, we tend to hate the idea of prospecting. The word *prospecting* makes me think of people digging for gold in the 1800s with huge pickaxes. To me, it sounds like work—hard work that's a long shot. Maybe you call it *lead generation*, which to me is an equally ugly term. Lead generation? No, thanks. Hand me the leads, but don't make me generate them.

As an agent, if you aren't finding people who want to buy and sell real estate, then you aren't in real estate. A client who chooses you because he or she has met you and spoken with you (and has not just been assigned to you by a computer) is a loyal client. It is much harder to earn the trust and loyalty of an Internet lead unless you are interacting with that lead.

When it comes to listing a home, we all put a sign in the yard, a lockbox on the house, and the property in the Multiple Listing Service (MLS). But what makes you unique? *You*. In real estate, what are you *really* selling? You! If you are selling you, then how are you going to sell *you* if you never leave your home?

Imagine an online or retail store trying to sell a toy. A picture of the toy is not available, just a few testimonials. There is no sample, no sign, and no box on the store shelf, just a sign saying that the toy will be magically shipped to the customer when he or she pays for it. What toy? Well, customers have the name of the toy, but that's about it. The toy never leaves the warehouse unless paid for. Is that how you run your real estate business? You have something to offer but only leave the warehouse and show off how great you are after someone hires you?

Prospecting is meeting people online, in person, and on the phone and finding an opportunity to show off how great you are as a person—easy to get along with, a bit of a bulldog when it comes to negotiating, funny, charismatic, easy to understand, good at explaining things, and someone your clients like to spend time with and trust. But in order for new people to see this side of you, you have to prospect. It's kind of like Internet dating; a photoshopped photo and clever lines won't cut it when you meet in person. You have to go out there, as yourself, as the amazing salesperson you are, and meet people. Call it prospecting, lead generation, whatever you want, *but if you aren't meeting new clients every year, then your business isn't growing. It's that simple.* Call it what you may, like it or dislike it, but get out there, and meet some people so that you can sell a few houses.

If you aren't meeting new clients every year, then your business isn't growing. It's that simple.

It won't be as bad as you think. How often would you say people move in your area? Every five years? Every ten years? If it's every ten years, then one in ten people are in their move cycle. So go talk to ten people. For example, in the DC metropolitan area, people tend to move every three to five years, so every one in five people are in their move cycle. Go to a restaurant, a metro station, a neighborhood, a PTA meeting—anywhere—and talk to five people about real estate. Hand out five cards. Do it every day, and you'll be surprised where your business ends up.

Chapter 4

ELEVATOR SPEECH

Every day, you have multiple opportunities to meet people and talk real estate, whether it is at a coffee shop, in a grocery store, or in an elevator. What we say does matter, and how we present ourselves can make an opportunity or break it. Just saying that you are a Realtor is a bad idea; it is not compelling enough to start a conversation. Someone might ask you who you work for or how the market is, but that's about it. A spark to turn this moment in time into a client relationship has not been generated.

How do you create that spark? You need what we refer to in this industry as an "elevator speech," a thirty-second compelling statement that leads to more substantive conversation that results in an opportunity to follow up and explore the option of the consumer or someone he or she knows becoming a client. As much as we like to wing things as Realtors, knowing what you are going to say greatly improves the odds of success.

An elevator speech must mention who you are, address a reason the consumer might need you as a Realtor, help assess the consumer's needs to determine if he or she needs you, and end in permission to keep in touch. This sounds daunting, but it's really simple.

1. Greeting
2. Body
3. Question
4. Close

Here is an example of what not to say: "My name is Sam. I am a Realtor, and I help people buy and sell. I just sold two houses this past weekend."

Although people want to work with a successful Realtor, there is a time and a place to share your success, and during the first introduction is not it. Nor is it the time to talk about how many awards you've won, how many listings you have, that you are a member of the million-dollar sales club, and so on. You need to say something that the consumer can relate to and that has a hook.

Ask yourself, why do people use Realtors in your area? What is their main fear or concern that drives them to our industry?

* Fear of not getting enough money
* Not knowing how to sell and buy a house simultaneously
* The preference of having a Realtor preview homes for them
* The fear of negotiating the contract and making a mistake
* The time it takes between contract and closing
* A prior bad experience when they tried to do it without a Realtor

Now ask yourself why people don't like Realtors.

* Perhaps they had or have a Realtor who is slow to respond to their calls.
* Perhaps they had or have a Realtor who negotiated poorly.

* Perhaps they have concerns that the agent is not working for them.
* Perhaps they are worried that the agent doesn't have their best interests at heart.
* Perhaps the house has been on the market forever with no showings, so they blame the Realtor
* Perhaps they are tired of the Realtor telling them to lower the price.
* Perhaps they believe that the Realtor is showing them houses the Realtor likes, not the consumer.
* Perhaps they are first-time homebuyers or sellers who don't understand the process and don't feel that the Realtor is explaining the process.

If you look at our profession from the consumer's eyes, then you will be able to come up with a compelling elevator speech that hooks the consumer because you are targeting a consumer's need, fear, concern, or thought. Some phrases might include the following:

* "I help buyers and sellers who are frustrated with agents who don't follow up promptly."
* "I work with first-time buyers who are anxious and worried about qualifying for a loan."
* "I work with frustrated homeowners who are concerned about selling their homes in these difficult financial times."
* "I work with homeowners who need to sell their current homes in order to buy their next homes and are anxious about the timing and process."

Chapter 5

MARKET KNOWLEDGE

If we are honest with ourselves, then we know that no one wants to hire a Realtor who doesn't know what he or she is doing. In fact, for new agents, one of their greatest fears is what to say when someone asks how many homes they have sold (I'll answer that later). But when we take a listing, we all have the same basic tricks in the bag: we all have lockboxes, MLS, color brochures, virtual tours, professional photography, and video capability. How do you differentiate yourself? You do so through numbers because numbers don't lie.

First, you need to know your market. Most agents don't truly know the market, so right there you can differentiate yourself. Don't believe me? Ask the agents in your office the following questions and see how many can answer off the tops of their heads. You should be able to do this if this truly is your profession. You will need to define your market by town or zip code or area. Go broad in the beginning; we'll narrow it down later.

1. How many homes sell in our market each month?
2. What is the average sales price in our market?

3. What is the sales price to list price ratio (original sales price compared to actual sold price)?
4. What is the average number of days on market?
5. What is the absorption rate for our market (months of inventory)?
6. How many homes are being listed each month?

All these questions are something an educated seller could easily ask, and the answers should just roll off your tongue.

If you don't know how to calculate the answers to these questions, then please see the addendum in this book. Knowing these answers will separate you from the other thousands of Realtors in your area. Show that you are a rock star by spending some time digging in your MLS and truly knowing your market.

Remember, the numbers don't lie, so use them to support your knowledge base *and* to support your efforts on pricing *and* to back up the numbers you get in an offer. Get friendly with your numbers!

Chapter 6

DON'T CONFUSE ACTIVITY WITH RESULTS

Now that you know what to say (your elevator speech) and have market knowledge to back it up, when do you say it? Every day, and it is called prospecting.

How do you prospect every day? You start by setting priorities and goals and telling yourself to do it. I recommend that you prospect first thing in the morning, before you check e-mail and Facebook.

Start your day by prospecting, and you will feel great once you have finished. I think there is a prerequirement for Realtors to have an aversion to prospecting, as we tend to procrastinate, postpone, and avoid doing it at all costs. And that includes the "cost" of putting money in our bank accounts. If we never ask, then we'll never get the yes. If we never tell people we are Realtors, then no one will hire us.

Start your day on time, with prospecting. It won't be easy in the beginning, but all the top agents will tell you they prospect daily. Set up charts and goals to reward yourself. Resist the temptation to do an easier task—just pick up the phone and do it!

Remind yourself that what you are doing right now will give you the financial freedom you desire. Some people find hanging pictures of items they want to buy helps inspire them. Others motivate themselves with pictures of their kids as a reminder of why they do what they do. Find your *why*, and focus on it while you prospect.

Your job as an entrepreneur is to find business, to find people who want to buy and sell. About one in ten are in the marketplace, so go out and find them, and connect with them. It's a numbers game that you have to play if you want to win as a Realtor. Make it a game, make it a test—make it whatever you need to make it in order to do it.

The key to reaching success as a Realtor and truly being in the top 1 percent is to create the habit of prospecting, and to do it every day, because no matter how full your pipeline is, a top producer knows there is always room for one more deal.

Don't think, just do.

According to Brian Tracy in *Eat That Frog*, successful, effective people launch into difficult tasks without hesitation. They remain focused on the task until it is completed. Close your office door. Don't answer incoming calls or e-mails; just make outbound calls. Think of it this way: you get paid only for specific results at a specific time—a settlement for a buyer or seller is when you get paid. Every call you make should be with the end in mind: How can I help the consumer buy or sell today? If you fail to execute or fail to go to settlement, then you fail to get paid. Is there any bigger motivation than that?

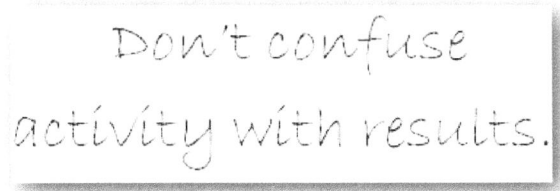

Don't confuse activity with results.

But don't confuse activity with results. Remember, meeting with your broker, talking by the coffee pot, and attending a sales meeting are just activities, not prospecting to put money in your bank account.

Chapter 7

MAINTAINING A DATABASE

Your most valuable tool is your database. Are all your past clients and spheres of influence compiled in one place? Where? On a piece of paper? An Excel spreadsheet? Most agents have a database here and there. You should exchange business cards with everyone you meet and compile them into a database.

Your database is the broth to your soup. This is the basis on which to build your business and to gain repeat business and referrals. I'll talk later about how to meet more people to add to your database, but in the process of adding to your database (soup), you don't ignore the broth—or the bread and butter. Imagine that we are cooking a full Thanksgiving meal. No meal is complete without the bread and butter, right? After all, what happens if you overcook the turkey? You eat more bread! Your database is your bread and butter.

Have you ever driven past a former client's house and saw a For Sale sign in the yard that wasn't yours? Has it happened with a neighbor? A friend? Don't worry; it has happened to all of us. We all know the feeling: a sinking in the pit of your stomach, that horrible, wrenching feeling followed by a burst of anger. How could they? The honest answer is they did because you didn't do your job. You didn't constantly remind them that you were in real estate and the best real estate agent for them. And why not? Most likely because you didn't have an organized database telling you to call everyone on a systematic schedule, a system to remind you to send regular e-mails and e-newsletters. Most likely, you market to your database in a hit-or-miss fashion, and in this case, you missed.

But today is a new day, and today you can start over and not lose a past client's repeat business ever again. Ready?

STEP ONE: ORGANIZE YOUR DATABASE

Put all your past clients and spheres of influence in one place. You can start with an Excel spreadsheet. Add a column so that you can label the contact (i.e., sphere of influence, past client, neighbor, school). This will save you time later on as you start doing more targeted marketing.

STEP TWO: FIND A CUSTOMER RELATIONSHIP MANAGEMENT SOFTWARE YOU LIKE

You need a system that will manage your contacts and allow you to categorize them, send e-mails and e-newsletters, and remind you to call them. And you need a system that will record all your activities for you. It doesn't have to be expensive. Check with your broker to see if your company has one (I know we offer more than one from which to choose). Customer relationship management (CRM) software can range in price from twenty-nine dollars a month to hundreds; they run the gamut from Wise Agent to Top Producer. The choice is yours, but pick one you will use.

As Realtors, we are creative sales people—visual people, not office managers. Getting and staying organized and practicing consistent marketing strategies can be difficult for many agents, making this seem like a scary task.

To help motivate you, consider the following statistics (remember, we always tell our clients "The numbers don't lie," and it's true for our business as well) on where buyers find an agent (according to the National Association of Realtors *Profile of Home Buyers and Sellers* 2015):

1. Referred by a friend, neighbor, or relative: 40 percent
2. Used an agent they have previously used: 13 percent
3. Visited an open house and met an agent: 7 percent
4. Walked into an office: 4 percent
5. Internet site: 7 percent

In other words, (Realtor speak), "referred by a friend, neighbor, or relative" means came from our sphere of influence—the very people we tend to be a bit hit or miss about marketing to!

In Realtor speak, "used an agent they have previously used" would be past clients. If you aren't keeping in touch with your past clients, then you just gave away 13 percent of your potential business. Let's say you did ten deals last year; 13 percent would be more than one deal. Let's say it was one deal: a sales price of $300,000 with a 3 percent commission of $9,000, and you are on a fifty-fifty split—that means you gave away $4,500 because you didn't keep in touch. Are you ready yet? Does a $4,500 return put a fire in your belly to get organized and get a CRM?

STEP THREE: BUILD YOUR DATABASE

Now add your church contacts, school contacts, and the like. Perhaps you are farming an area, so add your farm. Be sure to label each contact as you import it into your CRM.

STEP FOUR: GO BACK AND ADD MORE

> *If you are the listing agent, then keep in touch with the buyer who purchased your listing.*

Have you heard of adopt-a-client? This is where, *if you are the listing agent, then you keep in touch with the buyer who purchased your listing.* Add every buyer who bought one of your listings. Add every person who ever came through an open house (if you don't have those records, then we'll get there, but starting now, add every person you meet at an open house to your new CRM). In your farm area, do you have information on the absentee landlords and the tenants in your CRM?

STEP FIVE: ADD EVEN MORE

Go to YouTube to look up videos on how to export your Facebook friends' contact information and then start marketing to them. You can do the same for all your LinkedIn clients. Be sure to label all your contacts so that you can do targeted marketing.

You have a place to start now that you are highly organized and have a robust database with hundreds of names in it (and you know what to say). Now you are ready to start working your database. It's time to make some money!

Chapter 8

TIME AND MONEY

To be successful in real estate, you need to be committed. You need to come up with a plan, implement the plan, and stick to it. But this business is crazy, and one day you have so much business you literally are forgetting about clients, and the next, you are so broke you are eating your dog's food. Each deal is like a roller coaster, so when you get a few going at once, you feel happy and sick at the same time. When you have ten going at once, you can't remember your middle name and think you are superman.

The secret to staying sane and avoiding eating your dog's food is consistency. Stick to your plan. Create habits for your business and your life, and hold firm to those habits and the boundaries they create.

You need to be able to kick yourself in gear and to avoid procrastination (the biggest temptation we have in this business). Set your priorities for each day, and do them. Create the habit of writing down everything you have to do for the day (after you finish prospecting or the night before) and then rank order each item one, two, three, or four.

Items with a one are a must do, such as ratify a contract, counter, write an offer, or show houses. I like to think of those items as money-generating activities besides prospecting. Without these activities, we won't get to the settlement table, and if we don't settle, then we don't get paid.

Items with a two are those you should do, but if you don't do them, then the money still flows. For example, attending a webinar would fall into this category (it would be great to learn, but it can wait if you run out of hours).

Items with a three are things you should delegate. If it is a task that you can pay someone ten or twelve dollars an hour to do, then you should. After all, there are only so many hours in a day. Items that fall into category three tend to be mailings, e-card campaigns, e-newsletters and print newsletters, written follow up to online leads or expired listings, pulling expired listings, and pulling for sale by owner listings. As Jim Rohn once said, "Time is more valuable than money. You can always get more money. Try and get more time."

And then there are items labeled four, which are things we don't need to do or even hire someone to do but—if we were honest—take up a lot of our time, like watching YouTube, wandering the aisles of Home Depot claiming to get a feel for appliance prices, and chatting by the coffee pot.

As you complete each task, cross it off, or check it off. The human brain is designed to feel a surge of energy when it achieves an accomplishment. Feeling accomplished can come from completing a task or realizing a goal. The happier you feel, the better you will perform as a Realtor. The more positive you are, the more people will want to hire you to represent them. Feed your brain with check marks of accomplishments.

Did you know that completing a task can create the natural high that runners talk about? When the brain feels like it has accomplished something, it releases endorphins, which create a natural high that makes you feel positive, creative, happy, and confident. You don't have to go for a run to get a runner's high; you can simply accomplish your to-do list!

Have you ever heard successful people say that they enjoy their jobs? The reason is the release of endorphins; in fact, this good feeling can become addictive. Unconsciously, you will find you want to tackle tasks and finish them so that you feel good about yourself, and suddenly, you find you can accomplish more. You can put one more deal in your pipeline. You can make one more phone call. In fact, you may find it hard to stop after a while.

Go ahead: make a list, and start crossing off your finished items!

Chapter 9

FIND YOUR WAY

Successful people know why they are doing what they are doing. Sure, they like their jobs and are good at their jobs, but it is more than that. They have a deeper *why*. They want to be successful so that they can donate to a charity, win an award, support their extended family, start a charity, create scholarships, and the like.

You need to find your why. Why do you work weekends and nights? Sure, the pay is great, but let's be honest, the hours are crazy, and it is a lot of hard work between contract to closing, so what is your why? You need to find your why and focus on it. Making money will not be enough to sustain you in this business. You need a deeper reason to handle the rejection and the emotional roller coaster.

Find your why. Outline your goals of who you want to be and what you want to achieve, and write them down. The act of writing your goals down does something to the brain: it focuses on your goals. It's almost as if the brain is sitting up and saying, "Ah, now I see you are serious, so let's focus on this."

Did you know that most adults do not have clear written goals? *But of those who do have a goal, they accomplish five to ten times more than someone without a clear goal.* Ask a top producer what his or her goal is. That agent will know what he or she is working toward and where he or she is in terms of achieving that goal.

Once you have your why, hold on to it tight, and reflect on it every day. Every day, envision yourself as a successful Realtor. Picture yourself showing properties, going on listing appointments, and having clients sign paperwork. Picture writing a contract for a buyer, and *always* picture yourself smiling at the settlement table. And then imagine yourself doing your why—donating, giving, supporting, whatever your why is. After each thought of a closing and a paycheck, remember the why.

Ralph Waldo Emerson was correct when he said, "We become what we think about all day long." If you think about being a successful Realtor—doing the tasks that lead to settlement and money and thinking about accomplishing your why—then it will happen. If we continually think about something, we train our subconscious to do it, and then it happens.

Think about it. You are practicing what to say to a client. Practicing how to show a property. Practicing how to ask yes questions, which are questions that result in your client saying yes. Plus, you are envisioning yourself as a successful Realtor. With all that, is there room for failure? If failure is not an option, then don't let it enter your thoughts or actions, and you *will* succeed.

The brain is an amazing tool. It will turn you into what you tell it you want to become. You have the ability to learn almost anything (it may be at a different pace than others, but you can and do learn). Your brain is very adaptable. Your brain is easily influenced by the world around it and your thoughts and reactions to the world. Think positively. Focus only on being a successful Realtor. Practice the habits, skills, and abilities required to be a successful Realtor, and you will become one. Some call it "fake it until you make it," but I prefer to call it *practicing it until you make it*. Don't procrastinate, don't think negatively; just go out and do it! How do you do it?

* Call five people every day.
* Meet five new people every day (collect their contact information).
* Preview three homes a minimum of three times a week (this is what you sell).
* Vision your success (keep reading for more on this).

Chapter 10

POSITIVE THOUGHTS

Can you see it? Can you see yourself as a successful agent winning an award? Driving your dream car? Having a private office? Can you see where you want to be in twelve months?

"Before you begin scrambling up the ladder of success, make sure the ladder is leaning against the right building," Stephen Covey once said. And that is true for real estate. What kind of agent do you want to be? Commercial? Residential? REO? Luxury? First-time homebuyer? Condo expert?

Decide on your specialty and your target audience. Know your numbers. Now write down what you envisioned; write it in present tense as if it were twelve months from now. The following is an example, but make it your own: "I am the condo king and sell more than fifty condos a year. I earn more than $200,000 a year. I am the number one agent in my office."

The act of writing will cement the vision into your brain. Repeat these phrases to yourself at least fifty times a day. This will continue to trigger your subconscious to take the steps necessary to get to the goal.

Make sure you have a deadline for when this will happen. I like a twelve-month cycle, but it is up to you; perhaps you prefer an eight-month cycle. Don't make the goal too long. Remember, the real estate market shifts, so a goal of fifty deals this year may be OK but could be low if the market picks up in pace.

Also write down your marketing plan. What are you going to do to get there? How many calls? How many mailings and when? A monthly written plan will be easy for you to follow and eventually for your assistant to follow for you. Don't be afraid for your plan to build momentum. Perhaps in the beginning you will hand deliver the postcards, but plan in three months to make enough money to mail them. Be sure to write down that in three months you want earn enough money to advance your marketing.

You need to repeat your goal every day and make sure you are doing something daily to move toward the goal: prospecting, previewing, writing notes, networking, showing property, working desk duty, hosting open houses, cold calling, door knocking, canvassing, meeting people at an event, hosting an event, teaching a seminar, and the like.

The important thing is to dream big and write it down. This business is amazing; the more energy you pour into it and the more you believe, the more that comes back to you. But know that it doesn't usually come from where you expect it to come. For example, if you knock on two hundred doors today, then tomorrow a friend will call you looking to sell. *There is no direct connection, but your energy and positive vibe caused the business to come to you.*

Dream big, commit to yourself by writing down your goals, and believe in yourself. The bigger you dream and the more you believe, the more excited you become, and your energy and passion will

TARA WINFREE

attract more clients. Be happy, and be confident. Review your plan constantly, and adjust it as you become more successful. Don't stop pushing and reaching. *Don't become content, because if you do, then the business will stop.* When we become busy, it is easy to forget the magic of working every day and the daily repetition of our goals that got us to a successful place.

While you are in the process of setting work goals, also set some personal goals. Write them down, note how you are going to achieve them, and repeat the goals to yourself at least fifty times each day.

36

Chapter 11

TIME MANAGEMENT

Time management is not a Realtor's strength. We have a unique set of talents that allows us to talk to people and to translate their abstract and creative descriptions into a tangible home that they will like. It takes a special talent to comb through hundreds of descriptions in the MLS and to be able to truly identify which home your client may like. An equally unique talent is being able to compare a home when there is nothing to compare it with, and yet we can set a price that someone else will pay.

But time management is not usually one of our strengths. Perhaps it is because we live in a land of words and talking. We are visual people; we walk through homes for a living and try and help people envision themselves living in the home, and perhaps this is why time is elusive to us.

How many times have you sat down to check e-mail, and the next thing you know, three hours have gone by? Or you stop to chat at the copier and an hour goes by, and you have nothing to show for it? What about the "quick" showing—you know, "I'm going to just open the door and leave," but you stay for two hours. Or "I'll just call and leave a message," and you hang up thirty minutes later. How about, when looking for comps, it sometimes feels as if you fell into your computer and had an experience like Alice in Wonderland, and time has slipped by you.

Time. The clock is not our friend. Perhaps it is the twelve-hour days we work and how one day bleeds into the next—and one crisis slides into the next. Each contract is one step closer to more money, but on the other hand, each deal requires more work, time, and energy. With the ups and downs and the emotional thrill, time becomes almost senseless.

Where does the day go? To be successful, you must know where the endless pits that suck your time reside. What gets you off track more than anything? The best thing to do is to journal your time for a week. I know what you are thinking: you don't have time for that. The truth is that you don't have time *not* to journal your time. Until you know where you are least effective, you can't correct yourself, and you will continue running in circles. Successful agents time block, manage their time, and delegate. *But if you don't know what you are good at, truly good at, and what you just wallow at, then you can't be effective with time blocking or delegating.*

Start journaling, and be honest. For example, write, "Checked e-mail from 9:00 a.m. to 11:00 a.m." You don't need to detail every e-mail you read, but do record how long you sit in front of your computer in the morning. If you end up surfing the Internet, then record that. Many people find Facebook to be a vacuum for time. Do you pop on to post something and then lose thirty minutes? Journal your whole day from the moment you wake up until you go to bed. I once worked with an agent who consistently took a two-hour nap every other day. She initially told me she did it only once a week until she honestly started journaling. No wonder she wasn't as productive as she could have been!

It's OK to have downtime and time to go to the gym or to do yoga. You are not trying to prove that you are a workaholic, you are just trying to see that if you go to a sales meeting that lasts an hour, then you lose three hours of your day with socializing.

Remember that no matter how you manage your time, there will still be twenty-four hours in a day and sixty minutes in an hour. It is more about managing your actions than about managing time. *There will never be enough time to do everything, but there is always enough time to do the important things.*

There will never be enough time to do everything, but there is always enough time to do the important things.

Chapter 12

PLAN EVERY DAY

Now that you have time blocked, you can look back over your week and see where you lose time. List all the tasks you accomplished in a day and then go back through and rank order them one, two, three, or four. (See chapter 8.)

Now that you know what you need to do and where you get distracted, now what? How do you go from an abstract concept to reality?

The act of planning unlocks tools in your brain that will help you overcome procrastination and distraction. Did you know that every minute you spend in planning saves you ten to twelve minutes of your day? *Ten minutes of planning could save more than an hour and a half in your day.* What would you do with an extra hour and a half or, in some cases, two hours? Will you sell more, spend more time with your family, or pamper yourself? The choice is yours. Now that you know an hour and a half is on the line, are you ready to commit to the *how*?

Ten minutes of planning could save more than an hour and a half in your day.

Every night before you go to bed, write out your list of to-do items and number them in importance. You will most likely have tasks that you didn't finish from that day as well as new items to add. That is OK. While you sleep, your brain will become more focused on what you need to do. In fact, you may wake up with a great new idea on how to do something (market a tough home, do competitive market analysis for a home in the country, etc.). The longer the list, the more efficient your brain will make you. But don't beat yourself up when some items don't get finished and carry over; it's OK if this happens, and it likely will on a daily basis.

Always work from your list the next day. I understand that your phone is going to ring and that things will come up: you have to show a house or do a listing appointment or the lockbox is broken. Add it to the list, and take care of it. Turn your life into an action list, and be sure to mark off all the things you are getting done. (Remember the runner's high? The act of accomplishing activities releases chemicals in your brain that result in happy feelings.)

You should create different lists for different purposes. The night-before list is your to-do list for the following day. Also keep a master list of all your ideas and goals (don't worry about ordering or labeling it). Make a list for when you take a new listing. Make a list for when you start working with a new buyer. Make a weekly list of things you need to do for the week and a monthly list of things you need to do for the month (take continuing education credits, go to a ball game, etc.). There will be times when your night-before list has room, so transfer some items from your weekly or monthly list to your night-before list. For example, you may decide to call expired listings two times a week. On your weekly list should be to pull the information you will need to call the expired listings. When you have time, put the activity of pulling the information on the night-before list. When you have the information ready, put call expired listings on the night-before list. It is not reasonable to expect to manually pull the listings and to be motivated to call all at once (it's different if you are using a service to pull the data). Break the task down, otherwise, you end up spending the whole day working expired listings and get nothing else done. When you have a system, you'll find you pull the listings and scrub them one day and call the next (or better yet, pay someone to pull the data for you). Start your day with calling: pick up the phone and dial. Don't let yourself have the excuse of finding the numbers because something else will come up. Whatever you decide to put on your list, make sure you have the stomach and willpower to do it.

Plan each day, make a list, and organize your tasks. You will accomplish more and feel better about yourself and your job. You will get more done faster and have more free time.

Chapter 13

STRESS MANAGEMENT

Have you ever noticed that Realtors like to leave things to the last minute? Many will tell you they work best under a deadline. Some will be honest and tell you they lost track of the clock. Top producers always keep track of the clock in a contract, and they work efficiently to address the issues before the last minute.

Here in northern Virginia, we have until 9:00 p.m. to meet a deadline. But waiting until 8:55 p.m. to respond is a risky game: if your clock is off or something goes wrong, then you could miss your deadline. Too many times over the years, I have seen Realtors in a panic because they counted the days of the home inspection or financing contingency wrong. Know your dates and deadlines. The same goes for when a listing is going to expire; don't wait until it expires to call the seller. If you do that, then you most likely will be competing against other agents.

Working too close to the wire creates stress from the time pressure. Adding stress to an already stressful situation is how mistakes are made. In our business, a mistake could cost you hundreds or thousands of dollars. How about the home inspection addendum that went back and forth so many times that the buyer was about to walk, and the seller signed it quickly? The seller did all the repairs, but when they got to settlement and were asked for receipts, they had none to provide as they had done the work themselves. In the last-minute rush to save the deal, the seller signed off on a version that said all work was to be completed by a licensed contractor and that receipts had to be provided at the settlement table. The seller was livid that the agent hadn't pointed this out and that they had to literally pay.

I don't need to tell you that at 7:00 p.m. or 8:00 p.m., people get tired, drink alcohol, or watch TV. People do a lot of things at night, and being focused on the contract may not be one of them. I have seen deals where everyone signed via DocuSign at the last minute on an addendum to beat the clock, and the next morning the buyers and/or sellers were furious at what they had agreed to. Did they not understand because it was a DocuSign, or were they not of sound mind when they signed? I have no way of knowing, but I do know that when we conduct business during business hours we have less dramatic fallout and I-didn't-know-that responses.

The other challenge we run into as agents is that we tend not to allocate enough time to do what needs to be done. The conversation explaining that counter to our client takes longer than we anticipated; when we go to scan the document, the machine doesn't work; e-mail crashes, the printer jams, and the brochures don't print in color—it's always something. Our schedule gets backed up, and our panic rises, as we are cramming too much into the day as it is. Instead, allow an extra twenty minutes for every task. This way, you are building in breathing room. You know something will go wrong—it's the nature of the business—and this way you are ready for it.

Don't postpone the hard conversations. No one wants to call with a low offer, but the longer you wait and the more the other side is anxious to hear, the worse the call will be. Remember, it is not your fault; you are only the messenger.

Another call we like to postpone is the price reduction call. In fact, many agents hate this call so much that they would rather go silent and hide from their clients than make the call and address the elephant in the room. The longer you wait to make the call, the worse it is. In fact, if you wait long enough, then by the time you do call, the seller will simply fire you instead of reducing the price. That is not the outcome you want if you are trying to grow your checking account.

Instead, be proactive with your sellers. Even if you have nothing to say, call them every week. Report on the Internet traffic, and explain that the number of clicks on the Internet translates into the number of people who drive by a home, and that after people drive by a home, if they like the neighborhood, then they schedule a showing. We usually need showings to result in offers. Even though every year the number of houses purchased sight unseen has increased, most people still want to walk through a house, smell a house, and "feel" a house before they make an offer. No showings mean that the home is being eliminated based on location, upgrades, and price. Sellers can't change the location or neighborhood, but they can change how their house shows and the price. Share with sellers every time a home they are competing with comes on the market as well as the condition and price. Share when homes have gone under contract and your listing has not, and point out that the buyers chose to buy another home—in fact, they passed us by altogether. Ask the sellers what they would like to do to make the home more attractive to buyers. It is not your fault that the home is not selling, but it may be your fault if you are waiting until the last minute to educate sellers on a price reduction.

Chapter 14

80/20 AND YOU

I'm sure you've heard of the 80/20 rule: 80 percent of your success comes from 20 percent of what you do. Of all your marketing, 20 percent will drive people to you. Of all your clients, 20 percent will give you referrals. In other words, out of ten past clients, two will send you referrals. For every ten postcards you mail, two will generate interest. For every ten calls you make, you will get two people who are interested.

In your office, you may notice that 20 percent of the agents are doing 80 percent of the business. Believe it or not, this is true not only in your office but also industry wide. Why are 20 percent of the agents successful? The answer is consistency. Top producers consistently come to work, they consistently adhere to their marketing plans, and they consistently go through the 20 percent of activities that generate money.

It is about finding what you are good at, what you feel comfortable doing, and doing it over and over again.

Yes, they do the 20 percent of activities that work for them. I wish I could say their secret is doing open houses or cold calling, but I can't. Every one of us has a different skill set, so what works for one Realtor may not work for another. *It is about finding what you are good at, what you feel comfortable doing, and doing it over and over again.* As long as it produces the results you want, don't change it. It is so easy to get distracted by new products and shiny objects that will make our business better and easier, but only focus on the "new" if you know it will improve what you are doing. For example, Every Door Direct Mail for bulk mailers is a better use of time and resources because it can hit more homes for less money and with a larger product.

While most of us are trying to figure out what our magic 20 percent is that will generate the greatest yield, we procrastinate the most on the same 20 percent. The 20 percent with the highest rate of return is often the most painful, and therefore we avoid it. You have a choice: you can spend your time doing 80 percent of the activities that will not make your bank account larger, or you can buckle down and do the 20 percent that will. Top producers do the 20 percent; they focus on the why and on the benefits to get through it.

It is also important to note that when you have learned what your 20 percent is, you do not farm it out. Do not hire an assistant to do your money-making activities. If you are a cold caller and have success getting appointments and listings, then the temptation when you make enough money is to hire someone to do the calls for you. But the truth is that no one can call like you and get the appointments like you can. In fact, you may have a high capture rate for appointments because consumers can relate to you in person, just like they did on the phone. If you do hire someone and your appointments or conversions decrease, then switch back to making the calls yourself. Hire someone to do other tasks, such as gathering the numbers you will call.

It does get easier the more you do it. By doing your 20 percent consistently, day in and day out, you create a habit. Creating a habit makes it easier, and you become more comfortable doing it. Watching your bank account grow from your success certainly makes it easier as well. Plus, your mind enjoys working on a challenge, so once you dive into your 20 percent items, even though you emotionally may dread it, your mind loves it!

You can gain time in your life by focusing on the top 20 percent and discontinuing doing the lower 80 percent. One of the most powerful words in your business will be *no*. Sometimes you will say it to a client you suspect is not serious, sometimes you will say it to another Realtor in the workroom who wants your help, and sometimes you will say it to the office manager who wants you to help answer the phones. Don't be afraid to say no. In order to stay focused, you have to politely say no, and you have to set boundaries. *If you said yes to everyone, then you would not have time to focus on your 20 percent.*

I suggest that you apply this technique to your private life as well. Where do you get the most satisfaction in your life: watching TV or spending time with your family? If it is by spending time with your family, then you know what you need to do: turn off the TV, and focus on the family.

Let's now dive into what some agents do for their 20 percent.

Chapter 15

NO LONGER FOR SALE

L et's talk expired listings (I prefer to call them "no longer for sale" or "waiting for you"). The good news is that they want to sell; the bad news is that they are a little angry. And while many agents will try and get their business (making them even madder), only a few are good at converting expired listings. Why? Like everything, it takes a certain finesse, and some people can do it, and some can't. If you can't, then don't stress; there are other things for you to try.

The benefits of working with expired listings is that they want to sell; if you can prove you are better than their last agent, then the deal is yours. In the beginning, you may be competing with other agents, but like everything else we have talked about in this book, most of those agents won't follow up. Remember, it is unlikely you will be hired the first time you meet with an expired. They probably won't hire you the second time. *In fact, it could take up to five attempts to get a yes.* But isn't the reward of thousands of dollars worth the five attempts?

First, you need to identify the expired listings. Either set up a search in your MLS, or pay a service to provide the information.

Next, look at the listing to figure out why it didn't sell. It could be any of the following or something else entirely:

1. Bad photos
2. Inaccurate or insufficient information
3. Location
4. Condition
5. Lack of marketing
6. Price

Now that you *think* you know why it didn't sell, remember to keep an open mind. The most important thing is why the seller thinks the home didn't sell.

You will need a plan to reach out to the expired fourteen times during the first fourteen days. Why? Most relist in the first fourteen to thirty days, and you want to be the agent they choose. But they can't choose you, if they don't know who you are. If possible, call them (please be aware of the Do Not Call Registry), e-mail them, send mail to them, and drop by their home. If you have time, take a picture of the exterior of their home, then use it in one of your marketing pieces (wouldn't that catch your eye?). Remember, once is not enough. Twice is not enough. If you aren't committed to asking for the listing five times, then don't start.

Expired letter campaigns can be found all over the Internet. I also recommend a postcard campaign. Why not create (or ask your broker if they have one) a book for sellers on how to sell their homes? Be sure to include testimonials and samples of your marketing strategies.

When you knock on the door, what do you say? Obviously, you say who you are, and ask if they are still interested in selling their home. If they say no, then offer to set them up on an e-mail alert program that will notify them when a neighbor's house comes on the market or if homes on the market go under contract. Most sellers will agree to this, and now you have their e-mail addresses! Why will they agree? Because secretly deep down inside they still want to sell, but they are too mad to admit it right now.

Sometimes a seller will ask why you didn't show the house or if you showed the house when it was on the market. The answer is that you are primarily a listing agent. You specialize in marketing homes and highlighting features that buyers look for. You can spin this to say, "I am not sure why your home didn't sell. I imagine your previous agent didn't highlight some of the features in your home that buyers look for. Is there any chance I can see your home to determine if that is the case and give you some tips on how to sell your home?" In some markets, you can tell when a home is about to expire, and in that case, I recommend that you go see the house before it expires and leave your business card in the kitchen so that the seller knows you came by.

If you knock on the door, and they say they already hired another agent, ask them if they have a signed agreement. If not, then this is your opportunity! Ask them if they interviewed more than one agent. If not, then ask them if they would look at more than one house before buying it. Most likely, they will say yes, and you will say, "Like a house, not all Realtors are alike. We may have the same basic tools like a lockbox and a sign and the MLS, but there is more to selling a house than those tools. Do you have a few minutes when I can share with you what I else I do to market my listings? I sell homes for [insert your sales price statistics to list price ratio], or I sell homes in thirty-one days, and the market average is sixty-two days. Would you like to hear how?"

Sometimes a seller will be very hostile and blame the entire real estate profession for the failure of their home to sell. Be patient and understanding. Somehow you need to remind them that not all Realtors are alike. Perhaps you can tell a story from your life about a time when you had a bad experience buying a car or at a restaurant, but then you realized that not every car salesman or waiter was bad. In fact, you may want to tell the seller a story about a restaurant that had great food but horrible servers, and therefore no one wanted to go back, and eventually the restaurant went out of business. In this case, their home is the great food at the restaurant, and they just need to find a Realtor who will complement the home and provide good service.

> *Once you get the appointment, you will want to listen more than you speak.*

The key is to get the appointment. *Once you get the appointment, you will want to listen more than you speak.* An expired listing presentation is not the same as a regular presentation. You will want to ask several open-ended questions, including:

* "Why do you think your last agent didn't sell your home?"
* "What are you looking for in an agent?"
* "In your opinion, what is the most important thing an agent should do?"
* "What features do you love most about your house?"

* "How does your home differentiate from your neighbors' homes?"
* "Did you see any of your neighbors' homes when they were for sale?"
* "How did you happen to select the price you advertised your home for last time?"

I happen to love expired listings because I am convinced that sometimes in real estate it is better to be the second or even third agent. After all, if it is a stubborn client, and the first agent did it his or her way, and the home did not sell, then the client may be willing to listen. Also, the client will usually reduce the price for a new agent. We all know that everything sells for a price; it is just a matter of getting the price to a point that will engage a buyer to make an offer. As the second agent, you can often explain to sellers that you want to get an offer in hand so that they have something to negotiate. No offer means no buyer to negotiate with.

Your tone must be sympathetic and understanding. You should be able to show your value without criticizing the other agent. Remember that it is against the National Association of Realtors' Code of Ethics to make disparaging remarks about another real estate agent. Be professional no matter how nasty the seller becomes when discussing their former agent. (I have heard some amazingly horrible statements come out of a seller's mouth, and I just smiled and nodded.)

When you get the listing, keep the sellers focused on where they are moving to, not on the fact that the house didn't sell before. Keep them focused forward, and the process will be smoother.

Chapter 16

FACEBOOK

The advent of the Internet has changed the real estate industry. I am talking not only about real estate websites but also about social media. There are so many sites: Facebook, Twitter, LinkedIn, Snapchat, Pinterest, and more. For now, let's focus on Facebook. As of April 27, 2016, there were more than 1.65 billion users, which is about five new profiles every second (according to Zephoria Digital Marketing). With statistics like that, it's hard to find a good reason to ignore Facebook.

Everyone who joins Facebook has a personal page. Many agents create a business page. I recommend that you look for a local or online Facebook marketing class. Facebook is constantly changing and evolving, so I hesitate to get too specific, knowing that it all may change by the time you read this. As of the time of this writing, a business page is used mostly to post and boost ads. Business page content rarely shows up in people's feeds, so you will need both a personal page and a business page.

Do not post only business information. Do about three personal posts and two business posts a week on your personal page.

The business posts on your personal page should not be to the effect that interest rates have increased but rather more along the lines of "Congrats to Bill and Sue, who settled on their first home today!" Or "I was previewing homes and saw this view. Some lucky buyers will get to see this every morning when they wake up," and include a picture of the view. *Find something unusual or beautiful to comment on,* something that shows you are working but that is more like a cocktail party tidbit of conversation than a sales pitch. Keep your personality and charm evident in your posts.

You can use a system like Hootsuite to populate your posts and schedule them ahead of time. Many agents who are inconsistent with posting find it easier to sit down and do a bunch of posts or thoughts at once. You will need content on your business page and likely don't want to spend a lot of time looking for it. I suggest exploring the basic package of Engage121, which will e-mail you daily real estate-related articles that you can post to Facebook, LinkedIn, or Twitter with one click. After all, your time should be spent doing a money-generating activity, not looking for fun articles to post on Facebook.

I recommend that you Google what the current trend is for the best time to post to Facebook, as, again, this statistic keeps changing. As of this writing, engagement is 18 percent more likely on Thursdays and Fridays, according to Zephoria Digital Marketing. The highest traffic time is between 1:00 p.m. and 3:00 p.m. Interestingly enough, if you post at 7:00 p.m., then you will get more clicks than if you post at 8:00 p.m. Who knows for sure exactly when your posts will get the most clicks, but I do know this: if you aren't using Facebook, then you are missing out.

Learn how to boost an ad from your business page or how to create an ad. The technology on Facebook is amazing. Remember,

Facebook knows everything. People post their status (married, single, etc.), and if they include real information when they sign up, Facebook can gather all sorts of data, such as people's net worth and more. I don't know how they do it, and I probably don't want to know, but they can run targeted ads directed at me, and by golly if I don't click on the ads. And sure enough, Realtors have the same results: targeted ads for open houses or just-listed ads that actually drive people to the home. For a while, ads that said "What Is Your Home Worth?" were getting lots of clicks, and agents were capturing potential sellers' information. As of this writing, that ad is not having as much success as it was previously. Ads that promote the "Top Ten Things to Know Before You Sell" are working. You will need to play around to see what works in your area. If you aren't sure how to post ads, then ask your broker if your company offers any classes on the subject (if not, then reach out to me, and I'll come teach one!).

The great thing about Facebook ads is that you can post numerous topics to different groups of people for minimal funds. Once you capture people's information, you will need a follow-up campaign.

When it comes to posting on Facebook, don't be afraid to tag people (such as clients, if you are congratulating them). Post pictures and videos. Divide your "friends" into groups by how you know them, and reach out to a few in each category every day by liking one of their posts or posting on their walls. If you group your friends, then when you click on the group, it pulls up their activity, which makes it easy for you to peruse their content and make comments. More than likely, the group of friends is connected to one another, so a comment on one post may be seen by other people you know. Stay top of mind by posting enough, and always be positive in your posts.

Don't be afraid to leverage your clients. When you have a listing, send the seller a link for your brochures or videos or whatever you have, and give permission for it to be posted to Facebook and to other social networking sites. Remember, human beings need to be told what to do, so tell them it is OK to post the link, and they will (if you just e-mail them the link, then they won't necessarily think to post it).

For those of you looking to have a search site on Facebook or perhaps to offer a contest, look at HomeASAP. They handle the backend programming so that someone can search for a home on your business page. They also run contests and give away prizes (and you also have access to registrants' contact information), which you can boost or cross promote on a farm mailing. HomeASAP can also create your business page for you.

THE NEXT LEVEL OF FACEBOOK

Some of you are pretty savvy on Facebook already and want to take it to the next level. As previously mentioned, Facebook is a treasure trove of data, including people's contact information. Did you know that you can export your Facebook contacts? Why would you want to do that? To send them an e-mail, that's why!

I recently had a new agent extract her six thousand contacts from Facebook. We sent them an e-mail saying she was in real estate, and she immediately received seven responses. *Fifteen minutes of work brought seven inquiries. Can you beat that ratio with any other marketing method?*

Maybe you aren't new in the business, but this is still a great way to create your e-mail database (yes, people will opt out). How about promoting a community event like shredding old documents? Or collecting donations for the local homeless shelter? Perhaps you are having a mega open house on an amazing property. What about a reminder to change your HVAC filter? (Notice that I did not say to change your clocks; in today's day and age, that's pretty hard to miss.)

Let's flip the script, if you will. Facebook will also allow you to upload your own contacts and to run ads to those people. However, there are some caveats. First, this only works in Google Chrome. Second, the contact's e-mail address that you upload must match the e-mail address the contact has supplied to Facebook. Why would you want to do this? You can follow up with people you meet at open houses (run an ad just promoting you!). You can soft touch or subconsciously touch your database to help get your seven impressions. This last suggestion works great if you had been in the business but fell off the radar for a while.

For either of these methods, check Google for the most current directions, as Facebook likes to tweak the process from time to time.

Chapter 17

FARMING

I am a firm believer in farming, and I'll tell you why: it works. There are a few things to keep in mind in order to have the greatest success.

1. Consistency is the name of the game.
2. Less is more when it comes to words.
3. Do your homework.

I am going to work backward on this list. The first thing you must do is your homework. You need to find a neighborhood that works for you (not too far, a place you like, high turnover rate, etc.). I recommend driving around and seeking out areas and then going back to your MLS and doing a little research. You will want to run the tax records to find the total number of homes for the area/subdivision you are considering. Then you will want to pull the number of homes that have sold in that same area in the past twelve months. Then figure out the percentage of turnover. For example, say the neighborhood you are considering has 256 homes, and 11 homes have sold in the past twelve months. On a calculator, divide 256 by 11: the answer is .04, or in other words, 4 percent. That's not a great number, so I would look for another area. I do not recommend anything less than 6 percent. Anything higher than 10 percent is a gold mine that you should jump on immediately. Once you find an area with good numbers, look at the listing agents who sold the homes. Is one agent dominating the neighborhood? If so, then you may want to consider another neighborhood. I suspect there are more than enough neighborhoods and homes that you can find one with a high turnover rate that another agent isn't controlling. Why spend money in a David versus Goliath situation if you don't have to?

There are systems that now predict who is most likely to move in certain areas. Those may be worthwhile to look into, but they can't always predict death, love, and divorce. When I've had agents come to me with a proposal from one of these companies, and we analyzed the monthly cost to target only the top 20 percent versus an entire farm area (where you can pick up death, love, and divorce), they went with the entire farm area. You may come to a different conclusion, which is fine. I just hope you farm.

How big should the area be? I have read a minimum of five hundred homes, but when I started in the business, I began with about four hundred, all in a similar price range. Ideally, you want a variety of price ranges, but again, you need something you can handle, know, and be committed to. So start small, and once you see success, then you can start growing and adding other price points.

Depending on how many homes you select, it will impact your costs. Now is the time to research costs and decide if you can afford to mail consistently. Mailing once will not work; mailing twice will not work. Experts tell us that your name has to be seen seven times before it sticks, so be prepared to mail a minimum of seven times.

You should calculate postage and printing, and set the money aside. The reason more agents don't have success doing this is that they don't stay with it to see the results. Agents who stick to it will tell you it works, but it takes time. You will need to be patient and consistent to be successful with farming. It is rather like real farming: you can't just drop seeds and expect to see a plant the next morning.

There are some things to consider when getting pricing. Look at the quality and size of the postcard and whether it is in color. A postcard that is too small gets lost in the shuffle; if it's too big, then you are wasting money. I recommend color because it will catch the reader's attention. Ask your broker if they subsidize or offer a farming program. If not, can you print at your office? There are perforated postcards that allow you to run 8.5 x 11 sheets through a color printer and then easily break them apart. Another low-cost option includes Vistaprint.com. Something else to consider is postage. Will you be sending first class? Bulk? Every Door Direct Mail? Warning: Every Door Direct Mail requires a certain size (not a standard-size postcard). There are thousands of printers and options. Many local printers will design, print, and handle the postage for you (if you do Every Door Direct Mail, then sometimes the cost of the whole job is the same as first-class postage). I recently met an agent who was using the mailing service through *Clipper Magazine* (I have not tried this myself). However, in looking at *Clipper Magazine*'s website, we see the minimum numbers are probably higher than most Realtors want to start farming.

Now that you are committed, you are wondering what to say. First, place a logo, name, or image on *every* postcard. Remember the word *consistency*? It isn't just about committing to sending a piece every month or every two weeks; it is about your branding as well. Not good at creating logos and looks? Go to Fiverr.com, and you can hire someone to design your logo or look for you. Opening prices to hire someone start at five dollars. If you can't afford five dollars for logo design work, then this may not be the correct avenue of business for you to pursue.

Homeowners always want to know what their homes are worth. They go to Zillow, but the number is wrong. The local media tell them the market is up, and then the next day it's crashing. A tax assessment usually has no correct bearing on what a buyer will actually pay for a home. And while more and more websites are trying to correctly calculate these data for homeowners, everyone wants the information in an easy, helpful format. That's where you come in. Once a quarter, mail to your farm what is active, what has sold, and what is under contract. Make sure that you include the proper disclosures, and don't say that you sold the homes (unless you did). Make sure that you always include a call to action (the human being does not do anything unless told to do it)—Call Me Today!—or whatever you'd like it to be. (It could be something more fun like: Relax. Finding Your Next Home Is a Call Away.) Whatever you chose, remember to be consistent.

In the months that you aren't mailing the neighborhood activity report, what should you be mailing? Your goal should be to establish credibility by promoting yourself and providing information that homeowners may want. You could do just sold or just-listed cards showcasing your listings. You could do neighborhood tips—for example, when the pool opens for the summer and summer hours, a school calendar, a sports team calendar, or something else that shows you are a neighborhood expert. Promote a local event like a dog parade or where to go for the best Christmas lights. The options are endless. I recommend using a testimonial from a past client on every mailing. Nothing speaks louder than the words of someone they might know.

Use your farm area to build your e-mail list. Run a contest that asks people to register at a website or by e-mailing you. For the best results, you will need a good prize like a TV or a dinner for two at a fancy restaurant or tickets to a sporting event. I recently gave away a golf four-pack to an exclusive country club, and it had a lot of takers. The goal is to get as many e-mail addresses as possible so that you can supplement your mailings with an e-mail campaign, which costs less than print mail. Don't be afraid to hold more than one contest by trying to attract different types of homeowners (a prize that families may be interested in is different from a prize for a single person).

With farming, it is important that you pick your target. Become the expert. Make yourself visible. Give it time.

When you get your first listing, be sure to send a special just-listed mailing, and do an open house for the neighbors (see chapter 19). Put up a sign with your name and number. Use directionals with your name and number. Remember, your goal is to attain the greatest number of impressions in the shortest period of time. I know an agent who, when she got her first farm listing, sent just listed, under contract, and just-sold postcards. One day in the grocery store, a neighbor saw her and commented on how busy she was. The truth was that it was only one transaction, and the neighbor had not looked closely enough to see it was the same house; she just saw that the agent was busy. *Perception is reality.*

Don't shy away from absentee owners. Be sure to market to them as well to the tenants. Also, as properties become active in your farm area, be sure to preview them and know when they go under contract.

It is your job to know as many of the homes in the neighborhood as possible and what makes them different.

Do you really want to accelerate the farming? Knock on doors and introduce yourself. This will exponentially shorten the time before you generate business. Be the expert. What might you say? How about the following introductions?

* "I wanted to share with you what homes are selling for in the neighborhood."
* "I wanted to let you know that a home has come on the market in the neighborhood (or gone under contract or sold) and was wondering if you knew of anyone who might be interested in moving to the neighborhood?"
* "I just sold your neighbor's home, and we had more than one buyer interested in the home. Of course, we could only sell it to one, which means that I know of someone looking to move into this neighborhood. Have you thought about selling?"
* "I wanted to come by and remind you about the upcoming neighbor pool party (or whatever the event is)."
* "I wanted to invite you to a neighbors'-only sneak peek of the Smiths' home that will be coming on the market. The sneak-peek event is on Sunday at one o'clock. Do you think you can make it?"

Chapter 18

FOR SALE BY OWNER

For sale by owner listings are also known as FSBO; some agents call it the fastest and shortest business opportunity. In an ideal world, we want someone who is looking to sell his or her home and is motivated, and that is an FSBO. There is only one small problem with an FSBO: it is that they think they don't need a real estate agent. Those of us in the business know that isn't true. We know that buying or selling a home is one of the most stressful things a person can do; throw in emotions on top of that stress, and voilà: you have a pot of trouble just waiting to explode.

Working the FSBO market is one of the fastest and most cost-effective ways to generate listings. But let me warn you now that you will need some thick skin, and you must not be willing to take no for an answer. In other words, ask and ask and ask again. Most agents avoid working the FSBO market because they are afraid of rejection, but imagine, with the right training, do you think you could overcome an FSBO's objections and then get the listing? Of course you could.

According to the National Association of Realtors, FSBOs made up 8 percent of home sales in 2014. How many homes sold in your marketplace last year? If you had cornered 8 percent, would that more than feed your family and make your financial goals? Of course! Not to mention listings generate more listings, and they generate buyers, so we aren't just talking 8 percent.

What is the main objection that FSBOs have with using a Realtor? You guessed it: they don't want to pay commission. But what they don't realize is that according to the 2015 National Association of Realtors' *Profile of Home Buyers and Sellers*, the typical FSBO home sold for $210,000 compared to $249,000 for agent-assisted home sales. That is a $39,000 difference, so by hiring a real estate agent, the seller could make 19 percent more. Even after subtracting commission, the seller is usually ahead. Not to mention the fact that 87 percent of buyers used an agent in 2015 to purchase a home, which means that FSBOs must be willing to pay a real estate agent's buyer's commission. If the seller is willing to pay that, then what's a little more to pay the listing agent to net 19 percent more?

We know that buyers are online. They look at Realtor.com and other sites. Sites like Realtor.com only list property found in an MLS, which means FSBOs are cut out of a major search site. In addition, real estate agents (those who represent 87 percent of buyers) look in the MLS for property for their clients. Without an agent, the FSBO won't be in the MLS. Fewer and fewer homes are sold by signs and even less by print ads. The Internet is where the agents and the buyers are.

Most books you read will instruct you to call FSBOs, tell them you may have a buyer interested in their house, and ask if you can come take a look. This approach may work in some markets, but if it isn't working in your market or if you don't feel comfortable saying that, then why not try this: "Hi, my name is X, and I am a real estate agent with X. The reason I am calling is that I saw you were selling your home. Is it OK if I come by and take a look?" If they ask why or ask if you have a buyer, then say, "Until I see your home, I am not sure if I have a buyer. I am working with several clients, and I never know who I will meet tomorrow. Part of my job is to preview all the homes in XYZ town. Is tomorrow at two a good time for me to come by?"

This way, you aren't lying: you don't know if you have a buyer. Hopefully, you are previewing as much property as you can. (How else will you know what to recommend to price a house at or how much to make an offer?)

Once at the home, don't go for the hard sell. After all, only 2 percent of sales buy at the first meeting, according to MarketingDonut. com, so don't try and whip out a listing presentation (no bait and switch). Work on conversation and getting to know one another. Use open-ended questions, and listen to the answers.

1. "Where do you plan on moving to when you sell this home?"
2. "When would you like to move?"
3. "What happens if you haven't sold this home by then?"
4. "What are your favorite features of this home?"

Build a rapport, and offer to help. Present brochures or something else of value to sellers. Ask if they will give your name out to any buyers who come through the house who don't have an agent so that you can represent the buyers, even if they buy another home. Show your market knowledge. Ask how long they have been on the market and how many showings they have had. Then share your days on market knowledge.

Don't be afraid to ask what marketing methods they are using, and feel free to give suggestions like Facebook, video, e-blasts, or other marketing tools that you have found successful.

And then be prepared to follow up, to show your knowledge. If a house nearby comes on the market, then call and ask if they want to see it so that they know what they are competing with. (By the way, this is a good tip for any sellers who are struggling with the value of their home and their improvements: show them other homes that buyers will be touring that look better than theirs.)

Continue to talk to the seller during your follow up.

1. "Is the process of selling your home what you expected?"
2. "How are things going so far?"
3. "If you were to hire a real estate professional, what qualities would you expect?"
4. "Would it help to have a market snapshot of what is happening with other properties in the area?"

Follow up with a variety of e-mails, calls, and handwritten notes. Variety is the spice of life. You can take a picture of the exterior of their home and use it on the front of the notecard that you send— talk about adding a personal touch!

According to MarketingDonut.com, 80 percent of sales require five follow-up calls after the meeting. Most salespeople give up after one. Be the exception, and get the FSBO listing.

Chapter 19

OPEN HOUSES

Eighty-seven percent of Realtors fail in the first five years, according to the National Association of Realtors. Ironically, that failure rate is greater than that of restaurants. In fact, 96 percent of small businesses fail in ten years. The question is why is the failure rate so high when, as agents, we have a surefire marketing tool available to us: open houses.

Open houses are great. Buyers come to us. Sellers come to us. All we need is a good property that we market like crazy, and voilà: we have leads!

The key thing to remember when doing an open house is that only 1 percent of buyers actually buys the house seen at an open house. In some markets, I am told that percentage does tick up to 3 percent. But overall, whether it is 1 percent or 3 percent, that's a low chance of selling the home. But it's a great chance for you to pick up a buyer or a seller.

Which house you hold open will impact your results. I recommend that you hold an open house when it first comes on the market. The longer it has been on the market, the more likely the neighbors and interested buyers have seen the home (even if overpriced), so the following techniques won't work. If it is not your listing, and you can choose, then pick something in the midprice range for your area. This way, you get neighbors who might be looking to sell and move up (i.e., buy another home) and/or buyers who have a property they need to sell in order to buy.

Let's start with the obvious: picking up buyers. Be sure to promote the open house on all of the major websites, including Realtor.com, Zillow, and Trulia. We know that buyers look online and often will go to an open house before they commit to a Realtor. Another great way to promote the open house is on Facebook. You can run targeted ads to people "most likely to move," and you can select an area where they live. You can target either men or women. You can also target by marital status (separated, divorced, married, engaged), kids, and so on, allowing you to do extremely targeted ads at low cost. Done correctly, a Facebook ad can increase the number of open house visitors by nearly ten times. Don't be afraid to use video, e-blasts, and more. You can't tell enough people about the open house. It's a numbers game: the more people who attend, the greater chance you have of catching a buyer. Put an Open Sunday sign outside the property ideally six days in advance. Do everything you can think of—and then sit down and think of some more ways to promote the event.

On the day of the event, don't forget to saturate the area with Open House signs. The more signs the better. Top agents will tell you they will use between twenty to thirty signs. Strategically place the signs to catch people coming out of shopping centers, grocery stores, highway ramps, and so on, as well as to notify those in the neighborhood. The more signs, the better, but don't forget to pick the signs up when you are finished.

Another way to promote the open house to buyers is to mail (or do door hangers) to a "move-up" neighborhood. Is there a neighborhood nearby that is a logical move for a potential buyer to come from (maybe condos next to townhouses, as it's not uncommon to move from a condo to a townhouse)?

> *The other secret to success for buyer open houses is to be open one hour longer than the other opens in the area.*

The other secret to success for buyer open houses is to be open one hour longer than the other opens in the area. That way, when everyone else is closing up, and buyers want to keep looking, then you are the answer.

Now that you have completed the steps to drive people to the open house, don't forget to capture their information. Warning: George Washington and Mickey Mouse have been known to attend open houses. How do you get people's real names and contact information? Ideas include having a drawing for a gift card, having a brochure e-mailed to them, or having a contest to guess the price the home will sell for. Of course, you will want to ask if they are working with a Realtor, and invariably they will say yes. But don't just accept their answer. Instead, smile, nod, and ask, "Who is your agent in case I happen to know him or her?" And when they say they can't remember, smile and respond, "That's OK. I am horrible with names as well." Then make a note to yourself that more than likely they are not working with an agent. After all, wouldn't they know who their agent was if they did have one?

Be sure you have done your homework before the open house. Know what else is for sale in the area. As you ask people what features they like about the house, listen for the "buts"—"The kitchen is nice, but we wanted one with an island." Be ready to jump in: "If you like the area, then there is a home a couple of blocks from here for about the same price where the kitchen does have an island. Would you like to see it today?" When they say yes, tell them to meet you at the house you are holding open at the end of your open house, and you will take them over there. Don't give them the address because they may call the listing agent or another agent to show them the house in the meantime.

Most agents will stop there. That is what I call a buyer open house. The real money and opportunity is in this section: the seller open house. As you will recall, the National Association of Realtors tells us that *every time a home sells, seven people in a 250-home radius consider selling.* If you are looking for listings, then the easy fishing is at an open house (after all, you have a home that you expect will sell, which means that seven neighbors will consider selling). We also know that, once a home sells, two more homes will sell in six months. Why not be the agent who sells the next two homes in the neighborhood?

How do you do this? Host a neighbor open house but at a different time than the public open house. Perhaps you do the neighbor open house from noon to 1:00 p.m. and the buyer open house from 1:00 p.m. to 5:00 p.m. Mail postcards, put up signs, and even knock on doors to get the word out. Let the neighbors know that this is their time to come see the home's upgrades. (People are always dying to see what their neighbors have done to the house. They want decorating ideas. They want to see the improvements and even the not-so-great improvements.)

Although sending the open house invitations via Every Door Direct Mail sounds like a good idea, it is not. The thought of dropping to the whole neighborhood via postal carrier route for seventeen cents apiece postage is enticing—it's an easy way to hit 250 homes, right? Wrong. *If you send the invitation in an envelope that looks like a wedding invitation or a thank-you note, then it has a greater chance of being opened and read* (not a two-second impression like most postcards). The time it takes to open the envelope exceeds the two seconds that a postcard impression makes. If you use a fancy envelope, then don't put your return address on it. Nothing screams junk mail like an envelope with a real estate company as the return address. Use a real stamp (not a postage machine or bulk mail) and ideally hand write or print the address in a script font on the envelope (when was the last time you received a wedding invitation in the mail with an address label stuck on the envelope?).

Let your seller know you are hosting a neighbor open house because the neighbors may know of someone looking to move into the neighborhood. It is a good idea to serve food and to create a casual atmosphere so that the neighbors stick around. Be sure to find out where they live so that you can follow up, follow up, and follow up with them.

You should follow up with the people who come through the open house. Send them a thank-you card, add them to your database, and keep in touch. A crowded open house should drop lots of opportunity into your funnel of prospective business.

Possible questions to ask at an open house include the following:

* "What do you think? Do you see yourself living here?"
* "Are you working with an agent?"
* "Could you see yourself working with me if I found you the right house?"
* "Do you live close by or farther away?"
* "What don't you have in your current home that you would like in your next home?"
* "How soon do you want to move?"
* "How long have you been looking?"
* "Have you put in any offers?"
* "I'm going to be previewing these other homes in the neighborhood at four fifteen if you would like to go with me."
* "Here is a free pen. Will you please sign in?"
* "How much do you feel comfortable paying per month?"
* "Let's exchange business cards. This way, I can be your eyes and ears in the marketplace and alert you when something comes up that fits your interests."

Chapter 20

VALUES STATEMENT

Take the time to invest in yourself and to create your own values statement. Share the values statement with buyers and sellers. Let your values be prominent: hang them on your wall, and put them on your website, in your listing presentation, in your buyer presentation, and on your business cards. Commit to your values, and let the world know.

If you decide that part of your values statement is getting involved in and giving back to your community, then make a difference. Tie your charity work to real estate. For every follower on your Facebook page, make a donation to a charity. Tell people! Share your success on your Facebook page. Don't just talk real estate, but talk about your life and what you do and who you are. For example, "Like or comment on this post, and you'll be entered into a drawing to win tickets for a sporting event."

A lead generated by community or charity is the best type of lead you'll ever get.

A lead generated by community or charity is the best type of lead you'll ever get. These people want to work with you no matter what because of what you do and how you are involved.

Who you associate with is who you become. Make sure you are associating with people who share the same core values. Surround yourself with successful agents who believe in themselves. You will learn from them and be able to jump farther and faster. If you are the smartest person in the room, then you are probably in the wrong room. Surround yourself with excellence, with people who want to be the best. Find people with energy and passion that lifts you up. Make sure you are enjoying the ride of real estate; otherwise, don't do it.

When you are surrounded by like-minded people filled with passion, you will find yourself hungry for more. The competitive juices will flow, and you'll find yourself tackling new ways to do real estate.

Chapter 21

THE REFERRAL GAME

For the past five years, my financial adviser has always given me a gift at the holiday season—a calendar, pumpkin bread from a local bakery, name-brand cookies and a cookie jar, and the like. This year, I got nothing, not even coal.

In years past, when I asked why I got a gift, he always told me that he "likes to give a little something to his best clients." He let me know that not every client got a gift and that made me feel good. But nothing this year. What's odd is that I have "given" him more money to invest this year than in the past five years, so it's not the commission he makes off me that makes me his "best client." Perhaps he acquired more clients with larger accounts than mine, but it still seemed harsh to drop me as a "best client" when my account was growing. And then it hit me: referrals!

Every year over the past five years, except this year, I have referred new clients to him. Some years, I have sent him upward of five clients. I don't know how much they invested, but I do know that most of them use him for at least something (college savings plans, bonds, etc.). So the holiday gift in years past was for referrals.

He made a common rookie mistake when it comes to the referral game. If you don't reward my behavior when I send you the referral but instead wait to the end of the year to vaguely reward my referral behavior, then I have no idea that you want more referrals. Saying that I was one of his "best clients" did not tell me to send him more business; it just told me I was special.

As an agent, be sure to reward the referrer right away. Don't wait until the end of the year or the closing. Thank the person who sent you the referral immediately, and tie your thank you to the referral so that he or she knows that's the behavior you want and like. That way, the individual will send you more referrals. Remember that the size of the referral or whether you convert the referral is not what matters. What matters is that you were given the name. Not every referral pans out, but in real estate, it's a numbers game: the more people you talk to, the more business you acquire. That referral was an easy conversation to have, and it counts toward your numbers in terms of how many people you need to talk to.

Like an endless glass of lemonade, treat referrals the same way—as endless opportunities. What do I mean? Don't forget to thank the referrer every step of the way.

1. Call, and thank the person for the referral.
2. Call, and thank the person, and let him or her know that the referral went under contract.
3. Call, and thank the person when the sale goes to settlement.

But don't stop there. Let's say person A refers you to person B. In time, person B refers you to person C. The logical thought is to call person B and thank him or her for the referral of person C, but lemonade drinkers go deeper. They also call and thank person A for introducing them to person B who in turn introduced them to person C. Can you see how this might trigger a domino effect?

Chapter 22

THE WIDE WORLD

The advent of the Internet and the cell phone changed the way real estate is done. No longer are agents sitting by their home phones all night waiting for a call so that they can jump in their cars and drive across town to get a signature on a deal. Now it is done via DocuSign. The same goes for how people find an agent. No longer do they walk into a real estate office and ask to speak with an agent. The consumer asks a friend, calls an agent's cell phone from a sign, or reads an online review. But do they ever go to yourname.com as their first go-to? Probably not. They might Google hometown homes for sale, but it is unlikely that they will choose an agent by typing in firstname.lastname@yourrealestatecompany.com.

What am I saying? Have a good backend system for your website so that, when people Google common terms, your website pops up. Make sure your website is on every major site, such as Realtor.com and Zillow. Consider a name for your website that resonates with the consumer—something like RestonLakeHomes.com instead of TaraSellsReston.com. You want a website that tells the consumer what you do (features homes). You also want a website that people can remember, something that rolls off the tongue when you are at the grocery store telling someone about your website.

Your website will feature homes that are for sale. But remember this: most people don't click on a property to ask for more information unless they like it. And how often do they like the property? Less often than they don't like it—in other words, they usually click off and keep looking. You need something else to get them to click, something of value. School reports and crime statistics are all feasible, but why not some local history or information about farmers' markets and things to do? In the DC metropolitan area, we live in the land of homeowner associations, and people who are not from the area do not understand the true meaning of living in this type of environment. Think about a colorful blog about restaurants or a photo blog of places in your area. What shows you as the neighborhood expert? What tells people what is so great about your town? Why should someone work with you as a Realtor? Show them, tell them, and give it to them on your website.

Make the information easily accessible. Do one-click links to the topics just discussed as well as to types of home searches. For example, you could include a one-click link for downtown condos from $500,000 to $750,000. Or in my area, a hot topic is walking distance to Metro. *Once you have these pages on your website, you can promote them on Facebook and other sites.* Another idea is how consumers can get their closing costs paid for them. Try creating a place where people can sign up for useful real estate information, such as how to keep costs down when buying a home, why to get a home warranty, and other information along those lines.

Some agents have gone so far as to have a live chat feature on their websites. This way, if they are online or near their phones and someone has a question, then they can answer immediately. They promote that they are a real, live, local real estate agent and not a robot.

In terms of your website's layout and look, don't reinvent the wheel. The big guys spend a lot of money figuring out how to keep people on their websites, what information to supply, and in what order. I suggest mimicking their layout and format. There's no need to get creative; we want functional, not snazzy.

Remember that when it comes to local real estate, no one knows it better than you. Why not use all those statistics you pulled earlier in this book? Shine, and show what you know! Consumers go to Realtor.com and Zillow for the big picture, but they will come to you for the local picture. Be the niche market. Be the expert.

Chapter 23

MORE THAN PROSPECTING

Have you ever wondered what you do as a Realtor? Let's be honest: your number one job is being a salesperson. You are the boss of your own business as well as the marketing director, finance director, human resources director, contracts negotiator, secretary, social media guru, data-entry person, database manager, and more. But would you really need any of those hats if you weren't selling?

According to Brian Tracy in *Eat That Frog*, a salesperson's key areas are prospecting, building rapport and trust, identifying needs, presenting persuasively, answering objections, closing the sale, and getting resales and referrals. If I didn't know better, then I would say that Brian Tracy was talking about real estate, not sales in general.

We have covered prospecting in other chapters, so I will not discuss it here. We know that prospecting is key, and that without prospecting you have nothing, because you can't sit on your couch and think people will knock on your door asking you to sell their homes.

But we haven't spent as much time talking about building rapport and trust. It comes down to listening. It comes down to being involved, caring, and following up. If you say that you are going to call back at a certain time on a certain day, then you need to do what you said. It is about being responsive and answering as quickly as you can within reason.

Answering objections is about turning a no into a yes. What do they really mean when they say "Not right now" or "We need to think about it"? What is holding them back? What could you clarify or go over again? Where is the hesitation and why? Don't be afraid to ask the follow-up question.

What one skill, if you developed and did it in an excellent fashion, would have the greatest impact on your career? In contemplating that question, did you consider knowing what to say when?

Chapter 24

PRACTICE, PRACTICE, PRACTICE

Everything you do in real estate needs to be practiced. You should practice how to write a contract *before* you do so with your first client. You should practice how to fill in listing paperwork *before* you go on your first listing appointment. Read the contract and listing paperwork over and over again until you truly know it.

Every great athlete practices. Every great speaker practices. Every great actor practices. To become great at something, you must practice. You must know what you are doing.

You may have heard of Malcolm Gladwell's book *Outliers: The Story of Success* (2008), in which he talks about practicing for ten thousand hours to become a phenom in your field. Gladwell quotes neurologist Daniel Levitin who says, "The emerging picture from such studies is that ten thousand hours of practice is required to achieve the level of mastery associated with being a world-class expert—in anything" (40).

I am not telling you that you need to practice for ten thousand hours, and I am not telling you to become a world-class expert. But I am telling you to practice. *The difference between a well-thought-out, rehearsed, listing presentation and just winging it is the difference be-tween getting a paycheck and not getting a paycheck.* I have taslked to hundreds of top agents across the country, and I always run into a few who swear they don't use a listing presentation and that they just walk in and "wing it." But the difference between their ideas of wing-ing it and most agents' ideas of winging it is night and day. When you have delivered more than one hundred listing presentations, and you know how to overcome the top objections in your market, then you may wing it. You know the drill inside and out and can likely do your spiel backward. But most agents don't know the drill or even have a spiel, forward or backward for that matter.

For most of us, we have to start at the beginning. Read your com-pany listing presentation. And then read it again and again (at least three times). Then pick the pages you think you can deliver with the most impact, and start to deliver or present those pages. Think of it as writing a script, speech, or presentation. What visual will you project, and how will you phrase your words to have the greatest im-pact? Once you have decided, try it out on someone you trust, and let him or her help you adjust your verbiage (avoid slang and real estate jargon—for example, don't call it a listing). Now that you have your verbiage, start practicing.

When I first started out in the business, I was in my car a lot, driv-ing around town previewing homes. While driving to neighborhoods to knock on doors and canvass, I spent the time in my car practicing my listing presentation out loud over and over again. Like learning the lines to a play, I practiced when to pause, when to reflect, when to change my tone of voice, and how to ask a yes question.

The key is to practice. Be as smooth as you can before you get in front of someone. Rehearse, role play, and then go out there and do it. In the beginning, bring a presentation so that it keeps you on track and focused.

The same goes for showing houses and working with buyers. There is an art to this business. For example, when showing a house, if you walk into the bathroom first and then turn around and motion for your clients to follow, then the bathroom instantly feels dark and small. You want people to walk into the bathroom (no matter the size) one person at a time so that it feels large. In real life, do you ever have three adults in a bathroom at once? By putting three people in the bathroom, you made it feel small, and the clients can't compare it to their bathroom, because they probably have never been in their bathroom with three adults.

Practice the art of when to lead and when to follow. Practice how to ask yes questions to put a consumer in a positive, relaxed frame of mind. Practice asking open-ended questions and listening so that you hear what the consumer is *really* saying. None of this comes naturally, but with practice, you can train yourself to show a house a certain way and phrase questions in a certain way.

When a Realtor says, "Isn't this kitchen great?" the consumer may feel awkward if he or she does not like the kitchen. When a Realtor says, "I just love this kitchen, don't you?" and the consumer doesn't love the kitchen, he or she may not say so for fear of hurting the Realtor's feelings. A better statement could be "Is this kitchen about the size of what you are looking for?" It is a neutral question seeking a yes-or-no answer, and you can follow up by asking why or with a statement such as "Tell me what you like about this kitchen."

When you decide to become a top Realtor, you undertake the task of learning what to say. You must discipline yourself to practice until the skill set is fluid and natural and becomes a part of who you are.

Chapter 25

LETTING THE CLIENT WIN

Sometimes it is hard to let clients win. As their Realtor, we know that they are wrong. We know that the other side will not agree to whatever it is they insist we ask for. We know that what they want is not realistic. But is it worth getting into a fight?

Sometimes it is hard to let your clients win and do what they want when you know it is a ridiculous request. You worry about what the other agent will think of you. You worry about making the other side unnecessarily angry. For example, your buyer wants you to ask for one hundred repairs on a home inspection when the house has not yet appraised, and your gut says it won't. As the buyer's agent, you worry that the seller will be so mad that he or she will be looking for an out in the contract so that the price won't be renegotiated if the house doesn't appraise. But the buyer doesn't see why the seller would be upset when asked to repair one hundred items.

I want to caution you about arguing with your own client. Instead of coming across as knowledgeable and as someone with a lot of experience, clients often perceive you as conceited, fake, and manipulative. Over the years, more often than not, client complaint calls about an agent involve the client throwing out the phrase "So and so is only interested in making money and not in my best interests." I can also tell you that, in almost every call, I am thinking to myself that the agent is correct and that the client is wrong. But it is about communication, about knowing when to back down, and about knowing when to let the other side "be the bad guy" and say no instead of you.

It is OK when clients are upset to let them know that you are going to brainstorm several possible solutions and present the options to them later. Even if your brainstorm is the same thing you initially planned on saying, this gives the client time to calm down, and it implies that you care, you hear the problem, and you will come up with more than one possible solution. This takes you out of the conceited and manipulative position the client will otherwise see you in when you immediately say, "That isn't how we do it in this market."

When you come back to the client with several suggestions, present them in a positive light. Restate your client's concern and then discuss possible options and outcomes. To go back to our previous example of home inspection repairs, do *not* say, "The seller will think you are crazy and want out of the contract." A more sympathetic response could be "I understand your concern about all these issues, and we are going to discuss several options. I do want to remind you that the contract says items must be in working order, not new order, so it is a bit of a slippery slope. Also, many of these items could be repaired after you move in, and this way, you can ensure that the repairs are made the way you want. When a seller makes a repair, we have less control over how it is made, other than that a licensed contractor must do the work, and a receipt must be provided. I have seen some shoddy work over the years performed by licensed contractors, and I would hate for that to happen to you."

Do you see how the second approach guides the client to another option without saying that one hundred items are too much to ask for? (Please be sure to check what your local contract says in regard to the condition of a home.)

Did you know that during the Civil War, Abraham Lincoln managed to put on a positive spin when seven states had just seceded by pointing out that they had been friends before and would be friends again? If Abraham Lincoln can find the silver lining in the grayest of clouds, then I am confident you can find a silver lining and present a challenge in a positive light.

Clients can make us see red, but when they do, focus on the good. Remind yourself of when you first met them, when they found their dream house, or how they loved your marketing brochure. *Remember the good, and keep that memory in your mind while dealing with the ugly side.*

Every client will get ugly. After all, buying or selling a home is one of the most stressful things people do in their lives. It involves a lot of money, and they barely understand the process, contract, and fine print. In addition, clients are often getting married, divorced, having children, relocating, getting promoted or laid off, or dealing with a death in the family, which triggers their need to buy or sell. Their stress level is off the charts, and they take everything out on us, their Realtors. But we have to smile and be patient, if we want to make it to the settlement table and get a referral.

So breathe deep, tell them you want to explore some options, and call them back when they are calmer. Try to engage them in a dialogue. Most people calm down if they can vent what they are feeling and why they are so angry to a sympathetic listener. The key is to be sympathetic, considerate, authentic, and interested in meeting their needs. Sometimes we can't do what they want, and we have to explain that and say it in a way that they understand. Tell them that, if we could, we would move a mountain for them.

Chapter 26

THE LIE

There will be times when the other agent lies. The agent will say one thing but submit something else (this is because the client changed his or her mind, but one does question why the agent didn't alert you to the change). The terms of the counter are negotiated verbally but are written down differently. The home inspection that was supposed to be for big items only suddenly lists more than fifty minor repairs.

You know what I am talking about. The lie. The threat. The e-mail that makes your blood boil to the point that you are seeing red and want to reply in all caps that the agent should lose his or her license for stupidity. But you can't. Not if you want to make it to the settlement table.

When this happens (and it will far more often than anyone wants to admit because in almost every deal there is a "lie"; the question is, are you the liar or are you the one being lied to?), try to remember a couple of things.

* *Breathe.* At all costs, breathe. Stand up, walk away, and breathe.
* *It is easier to catch more flies with honey than with vinegar.* In other words, our egos can get the best of us, so cater to the agent's ego to get your way.

Instead of blasting the other agent and pointing out his or her errors, lies, mistakes, and headaches (as tempting as this is), try killing him or her with kindness: "I kindly request an explanation for [insert item], as I am sure that, as a respectful agent, you value your reputation and care about maintaining your credibility with your client, my client, and my real estate company." Of course, we all know that nothing verbal is definitive in real estate until it is in writing. We know that we are at the mercy of our clients. But there are times when it seems the other agent is pulling a fast one, such as increasing the sales price while you are midnegotiation, changing the commission in the MLS after ratification, or intentionally writing a vague addendum knowing the client is going to "squirrel" out of the intent.

The key is to make sure that we are always being ethical and on the up and up, that in the middle of the mud war, we don't sink to their level. It is easy to make a comment to our client that the other agent doesn't know what he or she doing, that the agent is a liar and that we have to do his or her job. But such comments are breaking the National Association of Realtors' Code of Ethics, and, with that, we are no better than the offending agent. It can be hard not to say anything about another agent after the transaction, but we must keep silent. Or how about when you have had a horrible transaction with Jane Doe and, on a different property for which you are the listing agent, you see that Jane Doe has submitted an offer? And yet you can't say to your new client anything bad about the other agent.

The lie happens. Sometimes we are forced into the situation, and sometimes another agent flat out lies to us, but it happens. Clients change their minds, and houses have flaws, but it is how we handle it as professionals. It is giving the other party the courtesy that something has changed and apologizing when it is out of our control. It is about asking politely for clarification when we feel that someone is trying to mislead us instead of getting into a battle of who can outdo the other.

Chapter 27

WHEN THE SELLER HAS COLD FEET

Every buyer and every seller goes through a what-have-I-done period, and it becomes a matter of how we handle it.

For sellers, they question whether they have hired the right agent. This happens after they have been on the market but have not gotten any offers. The longer they are on the market, the more they convince themselves that their house is worth more than the asking price and that it is the agent's fault that the house hasn't sold. Sometimes it is the agent's fault, but most times, it is something the seller imagines.

The problem is that, if we don't nip these thoughts in the bud when they first appear, then the thoughts become like weeds and choke out all sane thoughts in the seller's mind, and everything is suddenly our fault: if only they had another agent, then all (and I do mean all) their problems would vanish.

How can you nip it in the bud? First and foremost, when you take listings, tell the sellers when you will communicate with them and how often—and then do it. Nothing helps keep bad thoughts away than proof that we are doing our job: "Mr. and Mrs. Seller, I usually contact my clients on Tuesdays with an update on showings and marketing. Is this convenient for you? Would you prefer that I call or e-mail you?" This is the kind of dialogue to have on a listing appointment. But be sure you do it. The number one complaint sellers have about their agents according to the 2015 National Association of Realtors' *Profile of Home Buyers and Sellers* is that their agents didn't communicate. There is no excuse for not communicating.

What do you communicate? Everything. It is easy in the beginning.

1. Scheduled photographer
2. Wrote first draft of descriptive remarks
3. Scheduled stager
4. Ordered sign
5. Made copy of key

From here, you'll eventually meet with the photographer; another entry is that the photographs were uploaded into the MLS. Show everything you do every step of the way. Most customer relationship management software or marketing platforms have a form you can use to show your activity to sellers, but if you can't find one, then just use a Word document. Update it regularly, and submit it weekly. Here is a tip: don't try and do it all at once for the week. You'll leave something out or do it out of order and then your credibility becomes questionable. Include when a showing was and when and how many times you tried to get feedback. Show them that you ordered brochure reprints, and include that you mentioned their listing at a sales meeting. Everything you do becomes a line item.

Sometimes you haven't done some of these items for whatever reason, and the seller begins with the questions: "How many homes have you sold?" "How long have you been in real estate?" "Don't you think we should do X to advertise the home?" A client second-guessing us is the kiss of death. How do you respond? Always blame the market. You know what you are doing, but *there are several things you can't control, including what buyers want, and buyers can be fickle.* Although we know that real estate will sell in any market (even the Great Depression), what we don't know is what real estate will sell for what price. Buyers can change their buying patterns on a dime. One day, new construction is selling like crazy, and the next day, everyone wants a contemporary on the lake. The patterns go in waves of what is in. Is it retro? Urban? Water? Condo? Single-family home?

Usually a home hasn't sold because the price doesn't match the condition the buyer wants. It's hard to say, "I got it wrong," so instead say, "The market has shifted since we initially looked at the price, and it appears that fewer buyers are looking for X in this price range. That being said, we can still catch the market if we adjust our position to attract buyers' attention." There are statistics that can be leveraged to help support this argument.

But what about the direct question of how many homes you have sold? If you have sold a lot, then you can say, "I have sold X number of homes, and the buyers' desire shifts a lot. Buyers are fickle, and we have to catch them when they want your style home." The key is to blame the buyers. This way, it is not you or any other agent who can fix the issue. You can always say, "If we reposition your home to X price, then I am thinking of doing [another mailing, Facebook ad, etc.]." And the seller will say, "Why don't you do that marketing now?" The answer: "Marketing works best when we have a new hook. If you think about the advertisements for things that you know already exist like McDonald's, then they are either doing a value enticement ad or an upgrade. A value enticement ad would be a ninety-nine cent iced tea, and an upgrade ad would be that a Sausage Egg McMuffin now has two pieces of cheese. In real estate, the upgrade would be just that—an upgrade—since the home went on the market. In real estate, a value enticement is a price adjustment. Are you OK with a value enticement campaign?"

Chapter 28

DO ASK FOR IT

Jessica is an agent who puts a lot of time into her clients. She spends endless hours with them discussing home improvements, how tos, and what to do to get the biggest bang for their buck. While a client is going through the listing preparation process, she is diligent and keeps in touch to check on progress and to motivate the seller to keep going. She also drops off market updates letting the seller know what the market is doing and how that impacts the value of the seller's home. All of that is great but...

"It happened again," Jessica told me with a tear in her eye. The seller turned into an FSBO and left Jessica with nothing for her time, expertise, and effort. This time, the seller's sister was at a car dealership, the salesman mentioned he was looking to buy a townhouse, the sister mentioned her sister was about to go on the market, the car dealer came by the house then came back with his fiancée, and one thing led to another—ending with Jessica getting a call that her services wouldn't be needed after all.

I know you are thinking this would never happen to you, and I hope you are correct, but without a signed piece of paper, that potential seller is only as loyal as the word *potential*.

How do you protect yourself? Get the listing signed. What if the seller doesn't know when he or she wants to go on the market or what the price will be? No matter: get the paperwork signed, and put TBD (to be determined) under the sales price or list date. (Please check with your broker before doing this.)

If you make a listing presentation, and don't ask for the listing, then you have wasted your time and the seller's time.

You have to ask for the listing. As nice as Jessica was, the client had no loyalty to her, and Jessica had no protection. In this case, it was an FSBO, but it could easily have been another agent who had swooped in for the opportunity.

At the listing appointment ask, "Does everything I said tonight make sense?" If they say no, then ask them what you need to clarify. If they say yes, then continue: "Because everything I said makes sense, are you ready to sign some paperwork?" Some agents prefer to use a word or phrase like *John Hancock* or *autograph*—"Because everything I said makes sense, can I get your John Hancock on a couple of forms?"—or a more fun approach: "Do your fingers feel OK?" When they answer yes, continue: "Because everything I said makes sense, and your fingers feel OK, what do you say to giving me a copy of your autograph on this agreement?"

The tone or idea is a let's-get-started approach. Perhaps you would prefer to say something like "I feel I can get your home sold for X price, as we discussed. Would you please sign here so that I can get started tonight?"

If they say no to any of these questions, then that is OK. A no is an opportunity to go back over the areas where you were unclear.

Common objection: "We'll sign when the house is ready."

Possible reply: "I can see why that might seem like a great idea. But it does take some time on my end to get everything ready, so the fact that you're not ready tonight is probably a good thing. I need to schedule the photographer, floor plan designer, web designer, graphic artist, and more. Plus, I would like do a coming-soon campaign, but I can't legally market your property without a signed agreement. If you sign right here, then I can get started with my premarketing activities. We can put TBD in the agreement so that the home won't go live on the market until you say so. Does that sound OK to you?"

This tactic is saying that you can't legally do anything without a listing agreement. The reason they have to sign is not you, it's the law. (Blame someone else!)

Common objection: "We don't feel comfortable with the price."

Possible reply: "I completely understand how you feel. Pricing a home is hard. There is the financial side of the equation and the emotional side of the equation. Let's do this: sign the paperwork, but under price, put TBD so that we can watch the market a little longer to see the true value. Are you OK with that?"

Common objection: "We want to wait a couple of weeks because we heard homes sell for more in the spring market."

Possible reply: "Yes, that is a common thought. In our area right now, homes are selling in about X days. Come spring, the days on market genuinely ticks up a bit because there is more competition. The great news about selling now is that there are ready and willing buyers looking for a home like yours, but they can't find your home because it isn't for sale. If you wait until spring, then buyers have more homes to choose from, which means you may need to do more repairs to be competitive. So you may get a little more in sales price, but you will also have spent a little more to get on the market."

Another possible reply: "I understand that you are hoping the market will have an uptick over the next few weeks. The truth is that your home is only worth what someone will pay for it. As frustrating as that is, your home's value is dependent on your neighbors. By that I mean that your neighbor may decide to sell, and if he has a financial emergency, then he'll need to sell fast. He'll put his house on the market for less than the numbers we talked about tonight, and your home will instantly lose value. My advice is to sell while your value is strong and so that you can move to your next home without losing sleep over this house. Are you ready to get started?"

Common objection: "We want more advertising" or "We were hoping you were going to advertise in the *Washington Post*."

Possible reply: "My job is to generate maximum exposure to your home to qualified buyers. I love the *Washington Post*, but I am not maximizing your home's exposure to people who are qualified and able to buy your home. I invest my marketing dollars in online advertising, targeted Facebook ads, and mailings to move up buyers [insert your additional marketing efforts here] because I am looking for a ready, able, and willing buyer for your home. Does that make sense?"

Another possible reply: "My job is to expose your home to qualified buyers. Your job is to set the price at fair market value, a number a buyer will pay. And the buyer's job is write an offer and buy the house. Are you with me so far?"

Additional reply: "We'll know in the first fourteen days that your home is on the market if we have all done our jobs. If the price is right, and the exposure is correct, then we'll have online showings, followed by people driving by your home, followed by interior showings and then offers. If we missed the mark, then we'll know by our lack of results. Are you ready to get started?"

They may question how you know what people will do.

Answer: "According to the 2015 National Association of Realtors' *Home Buyer and Seller Generational Trends* report, more than 90 percent of buyers start their home search online. When they see a home they like online, 76 percent drive by the home, and 64 percent go inside the home."

Common objection: "We are going to sell the home ourselves."

Possible reply: "That is very ambitious. As a full-time Realtor, I am always learning new things because no two houses are alike, and no two transactions are alike. I am sure it will be a great learning experience for you. Have you read the Virginia sales contract?"

Whether they answer yes or no, your reply will be the same: "The first step in the process is to find the buyer. How do you plan on marketing your home?"

Answer: online, Facebook, flyers, open houses

Reply: "Great! I am glad you have the time to do all those things. Preparing the marketing materials and showing homes is a full-time job for me, and I'm not sure I could juggle it with another job, so my hat is off to you. By the way, did you know that 5 percent of buyers bought directly from an owner in 2014 nationwide? I would suggest you market to the Realtor community and offer a commission to capture the other 95 percent of buyers."

Here is another piece of ammunition for the FSBO argument: In 2010, for an arms-length sale, the median sale price through a Realtor was $200,000 for new and existing homes combined, according to the 2010 National Association of Realtors' *Profile of Home Buyers and Sellers*. The comparable FSBO price was $155,700. Avoiding the commission results in a sales price that is $44,300 lower than the $200,000 price that a Realtor can help to obtain—a difference of 28 percent from the FSBO price.

No matter what, wish them luck, and tell them that if they decide to hire someone because of the time, expense, exposure, or whatever the case maybe, that you will be happy to help them. More than likely they will come back.

Common objection: "My neighbors sold for X price, and you are telling me Y."

Possible reply: "You are correct that they did sell for more. Of course, that was before (name something that has happened in the news), which has left many buyers shaken. If buyers feel the need to hold on to their money, then prices decrease. While you and I don't see how an earthquake halfway around the world impacts your neighborhood, there are buyers and banks that do see an impact, and so we are left with a decreased value in your home. My advice is not to focus on your neighbor's home; it is what it is. Instead, focus on where you are moving to and what a great life that will be. We can't undo the earthquake or stock market dips, but we can help you move to your next home."

If need be, you can continue your reply: "The truth is that your home is only worth what someone will pay for it. As frustrating as it is, your home's value is dependent on your neighbors. By that I mean that your neighbor may decide to sell, and if he has a financial emergency, then he'll need to sell fast. He'll put his house on the market for less than the numbers we talked about tonight, and your home will instantly lose value. My advice is to sell while your value is strong so that you can move to your next home without losing sleep over this house. Are you ready to get started?"

HOW MANY HOMES *HAVE* YOU SOLD?

How many homes have you sold in this neighborhood? How many homes have you sold in this price range? These tend to be questions that make us freeze in our tracks. I am not sure why. I guess on some level we are afraid that if we give the wrong answer, then we won't get the listing. Yet I have heard of stories where agents were honest and said it was their first deal and got the listing. However, more often than not, those agents lose because of lack of experience, or so we tell ourselves.

How do you answer the question? One option is to rely on office statistics: "My team and I have more than twelve homes like yours on the market (be sure to look up your office statistics). In the past twelve months, we have sold more than X number of homes over XYZ price or located in ABC neighborhood."

You can always do a statistic out of all the homes that have sold in ABC neighborhood: "My team and I have been a part of 40 percent of the sales (or whatever the statistic might be) in ABC neighborhood." Doing it this way allows you to include buyers and sellers in your statistics.

Ask around your office to get ideas of support. In my office, an agent took a $1.3 million listing (her first listing over a million dollars in her career), and it went under contract in just three days. If you were in my office and looking for something to support your qualifications to list a million-dollar property, then you could say, "In fact, my office just listed a property very similar to yours in price and upgrades. We did the same marketing proposal for that house as I have shown you today, and it went under contract in a few days." Know your office inventory and the stories of the properties the agents are selling.

Other words that can work include: "I am confident I can sell your house because of my marketing plan and ability. My job is to expose your home to a maximum number of potential buyers and to

Realtors who have clients in this price range, and I will through very targeted efforts." Upper end properties don't want just anybody coming through, so explain how your marketing targets the affluent, not the looky-loos.

You can also throw in a line about how many homes you have sold: "Furthermore, having sold more than twenty-four homes in the past year is a testament to my negotiation skills and contract knowledge. At the end of the day, whether it is a $200,000, $2,000,000, or $20,000,000 home, they are all sold with the same sales contract, which is where I excel."

Be sure to ask for the listing, get the signature, and then begin your follow up. Don't be a Jessica, counting on a listing that never happens.

ADDENDUM

MARKET KNOWLEDGE

Are you ready to go deep into the math arena? Knowing the numbers will make a difference in your career. Ask a top producer what the market is like, and he or she can answer with numbers—and so should you. Take a deep breath; it will seem worse than it is. You will be fine once you get the hang of it.

1. How many homes sell in our market each month?
2. What is the average sales price in our market?
3. What is the sales price to list price ratio? (Original sales price compared to actual sold price)
4. What is the average number of days on market?
5. What is the absorption rate for our market? (Months of inventory)
6. How many homes are being listed each month?

All these questions are something an educated seller could easily ask. And the answers should just roll of your tongue.

HOW MANY HOMES SELL IN OUR MARKET EACH MONTH?

Here is a crash course on how to manipulate data extracted from your MLS. The first question of how many homes sell in the market each month would be how many homes actually go to settlement for a month. Run the sold data for the month prior to the month you are in. This way, you can say, "Sixty homes sold last month, and, so far this month, twenty-three have sold." Every morning, run the sold data for the current month so that you know where you are in the month. To be savvy, run the month you are in for the previous year. For example, if it is July 2016, then you would run sold data for July 2015. This way, you know if more or fewer homes are selling year over year.

How many homes go under contract and don't go to settlement is a different question, and, in fact, it is the last question on our list. Not all MLSs make this number easy to calculate, so you may want to drop this question depending on your MLS. Essentially, you are running the under contract listings with a settlement date for a given date and then, at the end of the month, comparing the sold data for that month with the first number. Let's say that sixty-three houses are under contract with a pending settlement date in July, but when I run final sold numbers for July (in August), it turns out that only fifty properties actually settled. In this example, only 70 percent of homes under contract actually settled (all the more reason to hire a good agent to make sure you get to settlement). But if you are running this number, be aware of a couple of things.

1. The end-of-month settlements may take a couple days to show up in the system, so if you run a report on the first of August for July closings, then the number may be different on August 5 for the same closings (unfortunately, MLS data are only as reliable as the agents inputting the information).

2. Some of the transactions may "push" versus fall through. In other words, maybe the lender needs more time for the loan, so the settlement date moves from July to August. If you are running numbers looking at pending sales versus closed sales, then you wouldn't necessarily know that the transaction didn't go belly up per se; it just needed more time.

You can still use the information, just be aware that the percentage could be slightly off.

WHAT IS THE AVERAGE SALES PRICE IN OUR MARKET?

To answer this question, you can run the properties that are under contract and find the average (add up all the sales prices and divide by the number of properties). This tells you the average price that the consumer is willing to pay. This is different from the average sold price (add up all properties that have sold and divide by the number of homes sold), which tells you the average price the purchaser is paying, and the seller is receiving. These are two different numbers depending on your market. In a hot market with a lot of offers on the home, I have seen homes bid up as much as $50,000, which means the sales price (action trigger price) is less than the sold price (actually paid).

To price a listing, you want to focus on the average sales price (also known as the list price or action trigger price), not the average sold price. Why? You want to entice buyers. Once a buyer sees a house and writes an offer, there is a level of commitment. If a buyer wants the home and finds out someone else wants the home as well, then the buyer is more likely to pay more to get what he or she wants. Let's say the home is priced at $500,000, and in a bidding war, it goes up to $550,000. The buyer still feels great that he or she got the home that everyone else wanted, and the seller is happy.

Let's take that same house and originally list it at $550,000. Buyers may not even look at the house because it is out of their comfortable price range. You could very easily end up with less or even no offers, so now the seller has to reduce the price. And we all know that a home with a reduced price tells buyers that there is something wrong with the house, and no one wants it. Buyers buy houses that they like and that they think other people also like. A home with a reduced sales price tells the neighbors that you, as the agent, can't sell houses. Don't overprice based on sold data; look at the under contract data.

WHAT IS THE SALES PRICE TO LIST PRICE RATIO?

The list price to sold price ratio is another interesting statistic. It tells if homes are being overpriced, underpriced, or priced just right. In my opinion, it is best to price a home just under the perfect price so that you can entice more activity. After all, everyone loves to think they are getting a bargain, and the more people who think that and write an offer drive up the price. To determine the selling ratio, divide the sold price number by the original list price to see the list price to sold price ratio. Anything between 97 percent and 100 percent is normal. Below 97 percent implies that the market might be shifting, and agents haven't educated sellers to adjust their pricing to match. See the preceding section to determine if your market is shifting by comparing active properties to under contract listings. Anything over a 100 percent ratio means a market shift toward a seller's market and that homes are selling for more than asking price.

If you are going on a listing appointment, and you know that the seller is interviewing another agent, and you know who it is, then run that agent's list-to-sales-price ratio. If the list-to-sales-price ratio is less than 97 percent, then more than likely the agent lets the clients set the price high and then asks them for repeated price reductions. If that is the case, then consider using this approach at your appointment: "Mr. and Mrs. Seller, it is important to me to sell homes as quickly as possible and for the most amount of money. My track record is to sell homes in X days, while market-wide, homes sell in X number of days. The homes I have sold also sell at X percent of the asking price, while market-wide, homes sell for X percent of the asking price. As you can see, selling fast and for the most amount of money is my specialty. If you are interviewing other agents, then I would encourage you to ask them what their statistics are. If the agent isn't sure, then I would be happy to run the data for you."

Notice I didn't say anything disparaging, but I showed that, as an agent, my numbers were better than the market, and I know that if I run statistics on the other agents, then my numbers will also be better. This way, you have planted the seed and raised the bar, and there is a good chance the other agent won't have a clue what his or her numbers are or even should be.

Sometimes the seller just wants to go with the other agent, in part because he or she has agreed to the seller's price, which you don't think is the right price. To address this, you could say the following: "Mr. and Mrs. Seller, would you be willing to ask the other agent if he or she would release the listing to me, if at some point the price is reduced to X, the list price I'm recommending? If the answer is no, then that's a sign that the agent may not believe he or she can sell your home for more than I'm recommending. If I were a seller, then that answer would make me uncomfortable." Another possible reply includes: "Mr. and Mrs. Seller, I completely understand. Can I ask you a favor? If that other agent asks you for a price reduction, then will you release the agent and hire me?"

WHAT IS THE AVERAGE NUMBER OF DAYS ON MARKET?

The average days on market is how long a home is on the market before it gets a contract. The shorter the time period, the hotter the market. Once again, take all the homes under contract, add up the days on market, and then divide by the number of homes to get your average days on market. No one has a crystal ball to foretell the future of the real estate market, but the closest thing we have is days on market. The longer the days on market tells us it is taking longer to sell houses and that the buyers are pulling back. When buyers pull back, sellers have to drop the price in order to get the buyers to engage. As the days on market extends, sellers may make enticements to the buyer or to the buyer's agent to make their homes stand out among others (I have seen cars offered to convey with homes as well as big-screen TVs, pool tables, agent bonuses, and more). When this starts happening, we call it a buyer's market.

On the flip side, when the days on market is shortening, and houses are selling fast, it usually is an indicator of a seller's market. The ultimate way to predict what a market is going to do is to compare active homes for sale with under contract listings. If more homes are going under contract than there is inventory, then it implies a shortage of inventory, which suggests a hot seller's market (homes are selling fast with lots of bidding wars). If you start to see the inventory and under contract numbers leveling out (you will probably also notice days on market extending), then it means the market is shifting to a more balanced market. A lot of active property with very few under contract means a buyer's market, usually with long days on the market and low prices (the buyers are not under pressure and have a lot to choose from). If you can put this in graph form and explain it to a potential seller, then you are bound to win the listing, because the numbers and the market don't lie. This way, you are explaining that you are not telling sellers what their homes are worth; rather, it is the market dictating the terms and price.

WHAT IS THE ABSORPTION RATE FOR OUR MARKET?

The absorption rate tells you how long it will take for all the homes on the market to be sold, if no other homes came on the market. If you are in a twelve-month absorption-rate market, then that means it would take twelve months to sell all the houses that are currently on the market, if not a single other home came on the market during that twelve-month period. You can use this statistic to explain to sellers how long their homes may be on the market based on different price points. When you do the math, you may find that the $350,000 price point is selling faster than the $360,000 price point. If the time difference is significant (twelve months or longer), then the seller may be willing to forgo the $10,000 price difference because of the time issue (after all, time is money).

How do you calculate the absorption rate? Take the total number of homes sold in your price range for a six-month period and divide it by six. That number is the average number of homes sold per month. Now take the number of active properties (the same criteria in terms of price) and divide it by the result of the first equation, and the answer will be how many months it will take to sell the inventory.

For example, let's say that a home listed at $359,999 will take 25.37 months to sell. How do we know this? In this scenario, four properties sold in the last six months for $359,999. When we divide this number by six, we get 1.66666, which would translate to 0.67. So now we know an average of 0.67 homes are "sold" in a month (that is less than one a month). In this same example, there are seventeen homes for sale with an asking price of $359,999. When we divide seventeen by 0.67, the answer is 25.37. That means that, if no other homes came on the market priced at $359,999, then it would take slightly more than twenty-five months for all those homes to sell.

Now let's figure the absorption rate using the price point of $339,000. Thirteen properties sold and closed at this new price point in the past six months. The price divided by six months equals an absorption rate of 2.17. Six properties are currently on the market at $339,000. We divide this number by the monthly absorption rate to determine how many months it will take to absorb what is currently for sale at our price point of $339,000. Six divided by the 2.17 absorption rate equals a 2.77-month supply.

Can you see how powerful this could be when talking to a seller? Imagine explaining the previous scenario and then asking how long they would like to be on the market: twenty-five months or a little more than two months?

CONCLUSION

There is an old Nike ad that hangs on my refrigerator that says, "All your life you are told the things you cannot do. All your life they will say you're not good enough or strong enough or talented enough; they'll say you're the wrong height or the wrong type to play this or be this or achieve this. THEY WILL TELL YOU NO, a thousand times no until all the nos become meaningless. All your life they will tell you no, quite firmly and very quickly. They will tell you no. And YOU WILL TELL THEM YES."

I hope that for every no, you are able to tell them yes like a rock star. I hope that the nos become meaningless when you hear them. You are meant to do this. You read this book, which says a lot about you and where you want to be. You have it in you to be a rock star— to tell them yes. I can't wait to hear about your success. Now get on the stage, be your own rock star, and have fun while doing it! And remember, you are the only one who can define your success and knows what you are capable of. So get out of your own way, and make it happen.

REFERENCES

Gladwell, Malcolm. 2008. *Outliers: The Story of Success*. New York: Little, Brown.

National Association of Realtors. 2010. *Profile of Home Buyers and Sellers 2010*. Chicago: National Association of Realtors.

National Association of Realtors. 2015a. *Home Buyer and Seller Generational Trends*. Chicago: National Association of Realtors.

National Association of Realtors. 2015b. *2015 Profile of Home Buyers and Sellers*. Chicago: National Association of Realtors.

WhoIsHostingThis.com. 2014. "Email Deliverability 101." Accessed November 25, 2016. http://www.whoishostingthis.com/blog/2014/02/12/email-deliverability-101/.

Campaign Monitor. "70 Email Marketing Stats Every Marketer Should Know." Jan. 6, 2016. https://www.campaignmonitor.com/blog/email-marketing/2016/01/70-email-marketing-stats-you-need-to-know/

The Top 20 Valuable Facebook Statistics—Updated November 2016. https://zephoria.com/top-15-valuable-facebook-statistics/

MarketindDonut.com "Why 8% of Sales People Get 80% of the Sales." http://www.marketingdonut.co.uk/marketing/sales/sales-techniques-and-negotiations/why-8-of-sales-people-get-80-of-the-sales

www.ingramcontent.com/pod-product-compliance
Lightning Source LLC
Chambersburg PA
CBHW070039210526
45170CB00012B/536